DESTRUCTION

How the **Democratic Party** & **RINOs** Almost **Destroyed** America

ZACH HACKERT

DEFIANCE PRESS
& PUBLISHING

DEFIANCE PRESS
& PUBLISHING

ISBN-13: 978-1-955937-69-6 (Paperback)
ISBN-13: 978-1-955937-70-2 (Hardcover)
ISBN-13: 978-1-955937-68-9 (eBook)

Published by Defiance Press and Publishing, LLC

Bulk orders of this book may be obtained by contacting Defiance Press and Publishing, LLC. www.defiancepress.com.

Public Relations Dept. – Defiance Press & Publishing, LLC
281-581-9300
pr@defiancepress.com

Defiance Press & Publishing, LLC
281-581-9300
info@defiancepress.com

This story is dedicated to the brave, hardworking, patriotic Americans who want to make a difference.

TABLE OF CONTENTS

INTRODUCTION

The Democratic Party, along with the help of a few RINOs (Republicans in Name Only), has enacted several terribly-damaging policies throughout the United States of America, all the while engaging in corruption to keep themselves in power. This level of corruption dates all the way back to the time just before the Civil War and the election of Abraham Lincoln, as the sixteenth president of the United States. The Democrats also were engaged in blatant racism, bigotry, and anti-Semitism that still occur to this day. While the RINOs were not engaged in those acts, they surely helped the Democrats enact their dangerous policies because they lacked the courage, strength, and stamina to stand up to the Democratic Party and fight for the American people as they were elected to do.

Yet, this is only part of the story. The establishment politicians from both political parties have assumed control and getting it back has proven exceptionally difficult. Former President Donald Trump accurately referred to those individuals as members of the "Swamp." The "Swamp" is nothing more than a bunch of DC establishment politicians and unelected bureaucrats that have been in office for decades. The "Swamp" has enacted policies that allowed the Italian Mafia in America to operate, allow Communist China to flourish, and allow enemies like North Korea and Iran to constantly threaten the United States without any repercussion, all the while getting involved in endless wars and failing to provide oversight to regulate government agencies. For example, the FBI has been corrupt since its conception and the days of J. Edgar Hoover. Where was the congressional oversight that could have prevented Operation Crossfire Hurricane? Members of the DC "Swamp" also enacted several terrible domestic policies like the Jim Crow Era laws, the xenophobic policies during World War II that led to Japanese internment camps, segregation in the South, reckless government spending that has led to a national debt crisis, and widespread government overreach and corruption during the COVID-19 pandemic, just to name a few. Not to mention the dangerous and idiotic policy of defunding the police and embracing socialism by the Democratic Party. Policies like these have almost destroyed this great country.

The dangerous and corrupt policies described throughout this book are policies that should never be repeated as we move our country forward. This story is meant to teach those who are willing to listen. While it does paint a dark, gloomy story, there is, at least, a silver lining: these policies almost always lead to a rise of Conservatism, which takes root at the heart of American values.

CHAPTER 1

The Birth of the Democratic Party and the Onset of Racist Policies in America

In order to understand this story, one must first examine the conception of the Democratic Party as we all know it today. But to do that, you must first look at how America itself came into existence.

Secondly, a vital question must be asked: if the people at the time fought the British during the Revolutionary War to win their independence, then why would the Democratic Party embrace big government policies like our European ancestors in the first place? It's a legitimate question, indeed.

Finally, the Democrats' blatant racism was on full display from the conception of the United States of America. As you can see, there is only one major difference between now and then, and that is the Democratic Party's radicalization in embracing socialism, which never works. This development wasn't observed until the 2000s.

In sum, these polices, while tragic, expose the Democrats for who they really are, and they can be used to predict their downfall if people can muster up the courage to reject them.

The Democratic Party as everyone knows it today originally came into existence in 1792 as the Democratic-Republican Party. It was founded by a few of our Founding Fathers, including Thomas Jefferson, James Madison, and James Monroe, who all eventually served as presidents of the United States. If there is one thing that they all had in common, it was the fact that they were from Virginia, which is highly significant for multiple reasons. First, Virginia was ground zero for all the slave ships being brought in while under British rule. Second (and take special note if you're a believer in Critical Race Theory, which is currently being peddled by the Democrats to indoctrinate kids), then you will see that it was all fabricated just to fit their narrative.

That is because people tend to forget about all the Native American tribes that were either kicked off their lands or flat-out killed by the settlers after they landed at Jamestown. Next, Virginia was also part of the Confederacy. Finally, Virginia embraced Jim Crow Era laws and segregation. Harry F. Byrd, who was a member of the Democratic Party, helped champion all of that. Byrd was clearly a racist. And not only did he serve as the governor of Virginia, but he also served as a United States Senator and was also the head of the Democratic Party in Virginia for decades. You see, that is a clear pattern of behavior that was established in one state alone.

The message from the racist Democratic policies is "Do as we say, not as we do." RINOs have never had the courage to call them out on it. Why is that?

Whatever the reason, the double standard has been tolerated for far too long—partly because the media refuses to cover it. The sooner the Democrats' lies and history are exposed, the better off the US will be because we could both learn and heal from it.

Now that you have a clear understanding of the background regarding the state of Virginia, you can clearly see why the Democrats' policies have been a failure from the start. Our Democratic Founding Fathers, while not perfect by any stretch of the imagination, do not deserve to be totally condemned for their actions. In fact, they did do some surprisingly good things—like drafting our country's founding documents, which conservatives live by. Those documents include the United States Constitution and the Bill of Rights, which represents the first ten amendments to the United States Constitution and guarantees civil rights just like those in the Magna Carta and the Federalist Papers. The Federalist Papers are important because they signal that for a healthy democratic republic to succeed, a single political party cannot call the shots, governing via majority rule. There must be bipartisanship and multiple political parties in order to achieve a healthy democracy. That's because the same people that founded both the United States of America and the Democratic-Republican Party embraced Libertarianism. That should have been everyone's first clue as to how radical and terrible their policies would be once they took power. This key aspect explains everything because it's an ideological belief that was developed over time. Understanding Left-Wing Libertarianism is the key to understanding the Democrats' ideology.

While many Libertarians tend to decry government

intervention, not all do. For example, Left-wing Libertarians believe in things like anarchism, socialism, racialism, and even communism. Knowing that should scare the living hell out of everyone. The Democratic Party was founded on these principles and beliefs. But Libertarians also believe in a key concept known as Federalism, whereby the nation has a centralized government. If you were to peel the onion back a little bit further and examine the countries that our Founding Fathers tried to mimic, then you would see that every type of government copied was either a Monarchy or an Empire. That is important because all had centralized governments, which explains the Democrats' quest to hold on to power. The proof is in the pudding. The Founding Fathers studied Greece, Italy, France, and Britain in order to form a new government after winning its freedom from the British after the Revolutionary War. Greece was used because of the Athenians, who utilized democracy well, but the Greeks, at one point, were under the control of Alexander the Great, who turned Greece into an Empire. Italy was studied for two reasons. First, the Roman Empire was a Republic, and the Founding Fathers liked the idea of a Senate like the Romans had. The second reason is that they like the idea of a centralized govern-ment that was utilized not only by the Romans but by the Catholic Church and the Vatican. Even though the Catholic Church and the Vatican are based in Rome, they operate independently and demonstrated their ability to operate a centralized government during the crusades. Finally, it is no secret that both Britain and France share the closest lineage with the American people. Both were on shore during the French and Indian War, and France was an ally of the colonists during the American Revolution and an ally of the Americans during the War of 1812. Even though Americans fought the British during both of those wars, the fact remains that the colonies originated under British rule. Both Britain and France were monarchies as well as empires.

Also striking is the fact that all of these countries had slaves at some point in history. You see, no one is perfect, but that should further put the practice of Critical Race Theory and "Cancel Culture" that the Democratic Party is embracing today to rest. As much as someone tries, they can't erase history. The embracement of Left-wing Libertarianism explains exactly why the members of the Democratic Party think the way they do.

The embracement of Left-wing Libertarianism ultimately enhanced the careers of a whole new breed of politicians that now thrive inside the Democratic Party. For example, the politicians that embrace this ideology call themselves democratic socialists, but socialism is just a form of authoritarianism. Adolf Hitler and the Nazi Party in Germany were socialists, as well as, the dictator, Nicolas Maduro, in Venezuela. So, how can the American people ever really trust politicians within the Democratic

Party that embrace these types of policies? The answer is "they can't" because the Democrats only care about power. What makes this trend even scarier is the fact that one of these politicians almost became the presidential nominee in 2016. But it was in 2018 that members of the "Squad" came into power. So, can Senator Bernie Sanders, Congresswoman Alexandria Ocasio-Cortez, Congresswoman Rashida Talib, Congresswoman Ilhan Omar, Congresswoman Ayanna Pressley, and Congresswoman Cori Bush really be the future of the Democratic Party, or will they bring about its downfall?

Some Republicans today argue that those individuals are, in essence, part of a shadow government within the United States. The silver lining is that since America is conservative at its core, conservatism will ultimately rise up and conservatives will be elected. It's just the question of when because it happens every time. The Democrats that embrace socialism are nothing but racist bigots that only care about power. They will eventually overstep their authority, and that is when conservatism will take over.

CHAPTER 2

The Ultimate Power Grab

Even before Abraham Lincoln was elected as the sixteenth president of the United States, the Democrats that controlled the Southern states came up with an insurance policy for them to get away for many years to come. That insurance plan was a coordinated plan of attack that resulted in states succeeding from the Union, the formation of the KKK, and utilizing domestic terrorism as a means to intimidate African Americans in order to hurt the Republican Party. This coordinated plan of attack by the Democrats brought the country to its knees—and for what? Power and nothing else. In order to fully comprehend the orchestration of this strategy, one must first examine the events of this period one at a time.

The 1860 presidential election finally exposed the Democratic Party to the American people for what they really were. There was a total of four candidates facing each other, including two Democrats. Those two candidates were Stephen Douglas, who was a supporter of the racist Dredd-Scott decision stating that African Americans weren't entitled to any rights under the United States Constitution, and John C. Breckinridge, who was a staunch segregationist and pro-slavery candidate. Now, Breckinridge referred to himself as a Southern Democrat, which was the faction of the Democrat Party that supported a pro-slavery stance. These individuals faced off against Abraham Lincoln and a third-party candidate. But since the northern states were both the most populated and against slavery, it was relatively easy for Abraham Lincoln, who ran as a Republican, to win those states, which were enough to win the presidency. The Democrats knew that because of their political positions, they couldn't win that election, so what did they do? They decided to change the rules by floating a crazy idea: What if the Southern states (and other states that supported slavery) break off and secede from the Union? They started floating this idea during the election. So, what happened? Well, after Abraham Lincoln won the presidency, those states that were run by Democrats seceded from the Union, which caused the Civil War. You can't make this stuff up because rather than changing and learning from a political defeat, they decided to tear the country apart. Fortunately enough, the Democrats underestimated both Lincoln and his top military general, Ulysses S. Grant. Their resolve stopped the South, which they defeated in a bloody war.

Since the Union defeated the Confederacy, the Southern states had to rejoin the Union. You see, this is why the Democrats absolutely hated Lincoln—because he both defeated them and forced them to change their ways. Abraham Lincoln paid a price for his courage and resolve.

Abraham Lincoln really pissed off the Democrats when he signed the Emancipation Proclamation in 1862. That document stated that slaves in ten of the states at war were free. While this was more symbolic than anything—difficult as it was to enforce—Lincoln chose to follow up on his proclamation by urging Congress to pass a constitutional amendment proclaiming that the practice of slavery was illegal. Now, that really infuriated the Democrats, who opposed the amendment. In 1864 the thirteenth amendment barely passed the United States Senate by a vote of 38-6 with all of the Republicans voting in favor and the support of only two Democrats. It had an even rougher time in the United States House of Representatives where it took two tries to pass it. That was because even though the Republicans were in the majority, they didn't constitute a supermajority, which was needed to pass the amendment. So, what did Lincoln do? Well, he certainly didn't give up; instead, he chose to campaign for his party to win the general election in 1864 by a big enough margin that would give them the necessary votes in Congress that were needed. Now, because of the Civil War and the fact that the South at the time was considered the Confederacy and not a part of the Union, it was relatively easy for the Republicans to obtain supermajorities in both, chambers of Congress. Congress then passed the Thirteenth Amendment, which abolished slavery in January 1865. The Union Army defeated the Confederacy to end the war a few months later.

Since the Union won the war, they could reconstruct the state governments in the South the way they wanted and force them to comply with the wishes of the Northern states in order to be readmitted to the Union. So, the writing was on the wall that the amendment would be ratified by enough states to become law. That really pissed off the Democrats to no end.

Well, a Democrat by the name of John Wilkes Booth decided to take a drastic last-minute step to try to prevent the Thirteenth Amendment from being ratified by assassinating Lincoln. But, by the time that occurred, twenty-one states had already ratified it when only twenty-seven were needed. So, Booth's actions didn't stop a thing; they merely delayed the inevitable by a few months. The Thirteenth Amendment became law after it was fully ratified in December 1865. The Democrats fought it every step of the way while Lincoln paid for it with his life. That should speak volumes. But the Democrats had a plan up their sleeves.

Shortly after the Thirteenth Amendment became law, a Democrat by the name of Nathan Bedford Forest formed a group of former slave owners with the purpose of terrorizing the newly freed black community into submission. That group became known as the Ku Klux Klan. This was nothing more than a temper tantrum thrown by the Democrats because they didn't get their way. It's really sad if you think about it.

Now, Nathan Bedford Forest, the KKK, and the Democrats made a critical mistake by underestimating the resolve of the Republican Party, especially

Ulysses S. Grant. They should have known better, considering that Grant had been handpicked by Lincoln to command the Union Army during some of the most critical points of the Civil War. Grant had also gained a reputation during the war as someone who didn't back down from a fight and someone whose tactics could be quite aggressive. Let's not forget that the same year the KKK was formed in 1877, Grant was appointed by former President Andrew Johnson to be the acting secretary of war. He was also considered a rising star within the Republican Party. So, why would the Democrats pick a fight that they couldn't win? Well, the answer is that the Democrats were a bit smarter than the Republicans were, and they were willing to be patient, playing the long game. Basically, their mission was to try to outlast the Republicans. Fortunately, it didn't work, but there were numerous speed bumps along the way.

By the time that Ulysses S. Grant was elected president of the United States in 1868, the Democratic Party knew that it was in trouble. That's because the Republican Party had already used the reconstruction laws to enact not just the Thirteenth Amendment but the Fourteenth Amendment as well. The Fourteenth Amendment states that no one can be deprived of life, liberty, or the pursuit of happiness. It also added a stipulation that states that if an elected official participated in a rebellion against the United States, then that individual could be barred from holding public office. Now, that was meant to prevent states from seceding from the Union in order to prevent another Civil War. That amendment clearly states that it can only be enforced by Congress. But Grant took things even further, pushing for the Fifteenth Amendment to be passed because he was tired of the Democrats trying to bully the African Americans via the KKK. The Democrats absolutely hated that, but they wouldn't dare try to mess with Grant. Why is that? Because they vividly remember Grant kicking the Confederates' asses throughout the war. So, the Fifteenth Amendment gave minorities the right to vote and considering that the Republicans freed them from slavery and gave them these rights, it was assumed that the minority vote would go to Republicans. That's why the Democrats in the South hated it because it would make it harder for them to win elections and stay in power. The Democrats were then forced to plot their next maneuver.

Since the Democrats thought so little of minorities and that no one had a right to tell them what to do, they used the Ku Klux Klan to harass minority communities in order to prevent them from voting in elections. The Democrats were even patient and conniving enough to wait until Grant was in the middle of his second term as president, which made him a lame duck president, to launch their coordinated plan. That was for each Southern state legislature that they controlled to enact voting laws that would target minority communities by making it harder for them to vote. These coordinated voting laws in the South became known as the Jim Crow laws.

The name Jim Crow came from a theater play that had a character by that name. But that the play was a racist depiction of African Americans. How sinister it is that the Democratic Party, who wrote the Jim Crow laws, now conveniently denounce them while scapegoating conservatives.

The Jim Crow laws effectively enacted the practice of racial segregation in the South. So, basically, minorities could only vote if they obeyed the segregation laws. So, how it is that Democrats were able to get away with this? Well, the Democrats found a legal loophole to work around the Fifteenth Amendment by looking at Article 1 Section 4 of the United States Constitution. There, it clearly states that each individual state can write their own election laws. They never said that minorities couldn't vote. But this was their way to suppress the minority vote in order to maintain the status quo.

Unfortunately, these laws stayed in place until the Civil Rights movement in the 1960s, but that didn't stop true conservatives from fighting to end those racist laws in courtrooms. For Democrats, it's do as we say, not as we do, and that needs to change. As much as Democrats may want to re-write history to cover up their racist policies by using critical race theory, but you can't ever *change* history. It's set in stone.

CHAPTER 3

The Start of Corruption in the FBI

The Federal Bureau of Investigations (FBI) has been corrupt ever since its conception. This has been the case ever since the 1920's when J. Edgar Hoover was selected to lead the federal law enforcement agency. But Hoover was by far the most corrupt individual to lead an American federal agency in American history. All you need to do is to examine the scandals that took place while Hoover oversaw the FBI. But those scandals and this level of corruption could have been prevented if it weren't for the RINO president who appointed him. He was in power for almost fifty years under multiple US presidents, who were all afraid of him. His legacy should be that of one, where the FBI should be viewed as having had a corrupt core of leadership that have persisted to present day.

J. Edgar Hoover was appointed by Calvin Coolidge in 1924 to lead the FBI. But back then, it was simply called the Bureau of Investigation. Now, we can see the irony in Hoover having been appointed to restore integrity to the chief federal law enforcement agency and to enforce the laws to root out corruption within the federal government amidst a corruption scandal from the previous administration.

Now, Calvin Coolidge became President of the United States after former President Harding died in office. But Calvin Coolidge was still a part of the Harding administration while he was vice president. Even that was amidst a huge bribery scandal that eventually became known as the Teapot Dome Scandal because it involved Harding administration officials bribing other state officials for the federal government to obtain land that contained oil reserves at Teapot Dome in Wyoming and other locations. To make matters worse, at the time of that scandal, J. Edgar Hoover was the deputy director of the Bureau of Investigation, and yet he did nothing about it. That was corruption at the highest level. Now, Harding, Coolidge, and Hoover were all registered Republicans, but true conservatives believe in the rule of law and small government. Those individuals didn't follow those conservative principles, making them RINOs. Those RINOs made it easier for future presidents, both Democratic and RINO, to exploit America.

As the director of the FBI, J. Edgar Hoover learned how to exploit his power during the Great Depression. This should not have been a surprise, considering that he was never confirmed by the United States Senate, was linked back to a corrupted president's administration, and the fact that the Great Depression spurred a great crime wave that swept through the country. During the Great Depression, famous bank robbers like Bonnie and Clyde, "Baby Face" Nelson, Alvin Karpis, and John Dillinger ran rampant across the country. At the same time, the Italian American mafia also operated virtually unchecked. This crime wave sparked public outrage to the degree where law enforcement agencies had to act to quell public sentiments. But there was a major problem. Hoover didn't want to admit that the mafia existed or was even a problem for whatever reason. Instead, he chose to order the bureau to go after the famous bank robbers, who were also known killers. That was a colossal mistake because a reasonable leader would have chosen to go after both. But considering that Hoover was a corrupt individual that didn't care about anyone but himself, his course of action wasn't surprising. The way that Hoover's agency managed the mafia is telling in many ways that should have revealed his true motives to the American people.

Organized crime has always been regarded as a secret society of gangsters that can extort anyone and everything as a means to gain power and money. Now, that sounds an awful lot like the way J. Edgar Hoover perceived things, doesn't it? Hoover let the mafia grow in power during the time of prohibition by choosing not to investigate and prosecute them. If it hadn't been for the United States Treasury Department agents led by Elliot Ness, then the mafia would have remained unchecked during that time. Hell, even state prosecutors had to fend for themselves without the help of the FBI, when they decided to go after gangsters like Charles "Lucky" Luciano, Dutch Schultz, and Vito Genovese. If it weren't for an ambitious prosecutor by the name of Thomas Dewey, who was just trying to make a name for himself, then none of that ever would have happened because Hoover wasn't going to do it.

Almost twenty years into his reign as director of the FBI, J. Edgar Hoover wanted to keep hidden from the public that the federal government made a deal with Italian American mafia so that they could protect the shipping ports and gather intelligence about the mainland of both the Italian and Sicilian peninsulas. Now, his allies would say that that deal was vital for the US military and allies' success during World War II. They say that because the mafia knew the terrain over there better than anyone, which may be true. But in reality, the mafia should have never been trusted because they were playing both sides against each other just so that they could operate free and clear of any government. It also told the mafia that if they were to get into legal trouble, then they could just make a deal with the government and get a slap on the wrist. This precedent of making deals with gangsters would later crop up when corrupt FBI agents made a deal to protect James "Whitey" Bulger and the Winter Hill Gang in the 1970s. That was also no surprise, as John Connolly came up in the FBI while Hoover was still in charge. You see, Hoover's corrupt actions spoke louder than words, and those who viewed him as a mentor followed the same corrupt path that he had laid out. But unfortunately, Hoover was just getting started with the amount of corruption and shady deals that he was about to propose.

Shortly after FDR ordered the roundup and

detention of all Japanese Americans after the attack on Pearl Harbor, J. Edgar Hoover wanted to take things even further. First, he decided to abuse his power by harassing, bullying, and intimidating people by ordering the FBI to open investigations on anyone they saw as a threat to them regardless of whether they had any evidence of the sort. Now, that sounds similar to when Louis Lerner, who was a Democrat appointee in charge of the IRS, decided to harass and investigate conservatives. Next, Hoover got FDR's permission to violate American citizens' civil liberties, which are protected under the United States Constitution, by conducting illegal wire taps.

And it got even worse when Hoover had Truman authorized the FBI's counterintelligence program at the beginning of the Cold War. The justification was that America needed someone to be on the lookout for Soviet spies, but they did not trust the CIA to operate within the US. Well, that was a gigantic mistake because from then on, FBI agents received specialized training so they could conduct spying operations. Now, critics will say that that part isn't fully accurate because Truman publicly denied the FBI's request. People have heard that line many times before, though, the argument never holds water. Those actions initiated the FBI's ability for them to conduct Operation "Crossfire Hurricane" in 2016. Hoover's FBI was the most corrupt organization within the DC "Swamp" and the rest of the world. But why was that? Because Hoover copied the tactics that the mafia uses in order to blackmail other world leaders and US politicians. Or to put it even more simply, it was because of one man's greed and lust for power. That is just unacceptable and completely inexcusable.

The only good news is that Hoover's downfall as leader of the FBI started in the 1960s—much to everyone's surprise. That's because the American people wised up and started to notice just how corrupt and incompetent his agency was. This occurred when people started asking questions about why the FBI wasn't thoroughly investigating or stopping the several high-profile assassinations that occurred. Those included Martin Luther King Jr., Malcolm X, JFK, and Robert F. Kennedy. Now, both, Malcolm X and Martin Luther King Jr. were widely polarized and popular figures during the Civil Rights Movement. Nonetheless, Hoover treated them like trash. Hoover tried to intimidate them every chance he got because he wanted to control them and their followers. While his agency was doing that, they allowed the Ku Klux Klan to run wild in the South. But unfortunately, that's not what did him in; it was his agency's inactions that resulted in the Kennedy brothers' deaths that did it. Why was that? Well, when a sitting president gets his head blown off in public—even when it takes place in a hostile city where the president isn't very popular and the FBI doesn't investigate it, what kind of message does that send? It wasn't a good one.

There weren't many people who trusted the findings published by the Warren Commission. Just look at how many conspiracy theories arose about that assassination, and then ask yourself if you understand the reason why the FBI didn't conduct a transparent and thorough investigation? Well, Hoover was a selfish individual that didn't give a damn about anyone but himself and didn't believe in transparency. But Bobby Kennedy's death was the last straw. He was the absolute front-runner to win the Democrat nomination for the presidency in 1968, and he probably would have won too. But all of that became moot when he, too, was gunned down.

These actions put together finally caused Congress to (try to) hold the FBI accountable and restore order by passing legislation requiring the FBI director to be approved via the US Senate confirmation process and serve for no more than a ten-year period. J. Edgar Hoover finally died of a heart attack in 1972, but the irrefutable damage that he caused remains to this day. Only a conservative president and a conservative-heavy Congress can fix that mess. The only to fix it is to root out the corruption, which spreads like a *cancer*. A president with a backbone would declassify everything, even if it's embarrassing to the FBI. Then and only then would the nation move forward and regain its trust in the FBI.

CHAPTER 4

FDR's Failed Legacy

Many presidential historians consider Franklin Delano Roosevelt to be an all-time great president not just for his leadership throughout the Second World War but for his government reforms that helped bring the United States out of the Great Depression. But that cannot be further from the truth, and it's misleading on several fronts. FDR was nothing more than a far-left socialist that almost brought the United States and the rest of the world to ruin.

FDR was originally elected as president of the United States in 1932 on the sole promise that he would manage America's financial situation better and help the US escape the Great Depression that was ravaging the country at the time. So, to keep this promise, he proposed the New Deal to America. That was nothing more than an expansion of government and government overreach, plain and simple. No one should be surprised by just how corrupt this plan was—if they would just take the time and examine the coalition of voters that put FDR in office, to begin with. FDR's coalition of voters consisted of socialists, labor unions, poor Southern whites, minorities, liberals, and even communists. Now, considering that FDR won the presidency by a landslide in all four of his elections, one might assume that this was the mainstream way of thinking in the United States, but that cannot be further from the truth.

When he was elected as president in 1932, America was exactly three years into the depression, and that put a third of all Americans out of work. Others were struggling financially, so many people prioritized simple survival and fending for their families. Just look at how people received the news during that time: televisions weren't out yet, and radios were expensive, so that left newspapers. Were the American people as informed about a political candidate running for office, as they are today? The answer is no, they were not.

Now, there is one more important question that deserves an answer when it comes to FDR's rise to power during the Great Depression: Just how many people voted in the presidential elections in 1932, 1936, and 1940? In the 1930s, the United States had a population of 122,775,046, but of that amount of people, roughly 38.5 million people voted in the 1932 presidential election. That means that two/thirds of the American people didn't vote during the 1932 presidential election. The country only did slightly better in 1936, but still, only 36 percent of the country participated in the election. Only 37 percent of the country voted in the 1940 presidential election. So, of those three elections, at least three-fifths of the country didn't vote because they were more focused on personal issues. So, FDR's policies were never mainstream. The Republican Party also nominated serval bad candidates to face him. With all this being said, FDR still pushed his corrupt policies onto the American people after winning the presidency.

FDR's New Deal was his plan to help the United States recover from the Great Depression. This was eventually broken up into two separate pieces of major legislation. It was solely designed to implement what became known as the 3 Rs, which were to recover the economy, provide relief to the poor and those who had lost their jobs, and reform the financial situation. Now, given FDR's aims (and the people he had to appease), this should have scared the living hell out of everyone, as the "plan" involved the redistribution of wealth and higher taxes for the wealthy. But socialist policies never work. So, what FDR and the Democrats that controlled Congress decided to do was fool the American people by attempting to gain their trust by passing reforms designed to give relief to those in need right away and to put people back to work. To do this, FDR and the Democrats had to expand the current level of bureaucracy so they could have government agencies running these programs. The American people absolutely hate dealing with bureaucratic red tape because it takes a long time and it's confusing to most. FDR's administration even put a massive number of regulations in place for these government agencies and work programs to operate. That was a colossal mistake because what we learn from Donald Trump's administration and even Ronald Reagan's administration is that less government is key to a vibrant economy. Two of the government agencies that FDR used to enact this legislation were the

Public Works Administration (PWA) and the Civilian Conservation Corps (CCC). They were designed to create jobs and build up the US infrastructure, which seem like a clever idea on the surface but then came the second part of the New Deal.

The second part of the New Deal was one of the most corrupt pieces of legislation ever passed by Congress. Its sole purpose was to appease the communists and socialists within FDR's political base. After earning the trust of the American people by passing the first part of the New Deal, the Democrats decided that no one would notice and that they could muscle through the second part of the New Deal to get it passed. The legislation itself raised taxes on everyone by instituting a wealth tax, with the sole purpose of redistributing money across America. Now, why does this sound familiar? Oh, that's right: the socialists in Congress today are pushing for the exact same thing. This piece of legislation even went further than that because it enacted the Social Security Act, which created the current welfare system, and it also produced the Wagner Act. Well, according to the first part of the New Deal, the unemployment benefits enacted were only supposed to be temporary and provide immediate relief, but when the Social Security Act was passed, those benefits became permanent. The reason that they were originally temporary had something to do with the question of funding. If they were permanent, how would Congress pay for it, especially with the country hurting financially during the depression? The Democrats decided that it would be paid for through taxes. So, a third of the country was out of work and others were struggling financially, so their solution was to raise taxes. That's smart.

The Democrats have gradually made the Social Security Act more permanent by adding Medicaid and Medicare to it. But all it did was raise taxes and expand the bureaucracy to unprecedented levels, which average Americans despise. The Wagner Act created the National Labor Relations Board, which sounds harmless, but it was meant to solidify labor unions' power across the country. The problem with that is that Labor unions tend to support Democratic candidates. So, it was a kick-back to the union heads with taxpayer money, to solidify a permanent Democratic majority. You can't make this stuff up. It was corruption at the highest levels. If that isn't bad enough, the Democrats tried to pack the United States Supreme Court, just like they are today, so they would have justices on the court that they thought would be friendly to their policies. Instead of packing the court, FDR appointed justices (when seats were open) that were friendlier to Democratic policies. All this did was alienate conservative democrats. The New Deal, when fully implemented, eventually led to an economic recession in 1938. So, it did nothing to end the depression.

The depression didn't end until the start of the

Second World War. How do we know that it was the Second World War that ended the Great Depression and not FDR's New Deal? Because war is the biggest business. Just look at how many factories came to life to produce military equipment—not to mention the number of servicemembers needed to serve during the war. Every servicemember of the military gets paid by the federal government. That's millions of jobs that were created. The money that people made was spent in stores, which helped to juice the economy even more. Without the Second World War, the Great Depression could have lasted for a few more years, which is terrible. FDR became president in 1933 and the United States didn't enter the Second World War until December of 1941, so that's two full terms that FDR was in office while the depression continued ravaging the country. FDR was a failure, and he should have left office in disgrace.

In 1940, Franklin Delano Roosevelt made the ultimate power grab by ignoring precedent and deciding to run for a third term as president of the United States. Until that time, that had never been done before. Hell, not even George Washington attempted to do such a thing even though he was widely popular. He stated that he didn't think that a US President should serve more than two terms in office because shorter terms would allow other leaders an opportunity, and he feared that if a president ever served more than that, then they would be perceived as a king, thus weakening our institutions.

Nonetheless, FDR ignored this precedent and ran for a third term anyway. So, why did FDR do this? The answer is that he was nothing more than a far-left radical socialist who was obsessed with power. He succeeded because he exploited that time period to his advantage. He didn't care if his policies weren't the mainstream, and he also didn't even try to reach across the political isle to have bipartisanship. Even a member of his own party compared him to Karl Marx and Vladimir Lenin, two revered leaders of the communist movement. But once FDR was re-elected for a third term as president of the United States, he made even more horrendous decisions that put not only the United States but the entire world on the brink of ruin. Those decisions included the events that led up to the United States' involvement in the Second World War and those made during the war.

FDR's actions leading up to the US involvement in the war were a combination of dereliction of duty and incompetence. First, he decided to weaken defenses in the Pacific fleet by transferring warships to the Atlantic as a precaution against German aggression. That was a massive mistake that came with major ramifications. Being president of the United States, he had access to national security and intelligence briefings, which should have been told to be on the lookout for Japanese military aggression. So, in essence, he made the US Naval Base at Pearl Harbor more vulnerable to attack.

FDR should have learned from the previous World War that if the United States were to aid its European allies, then it would make them more susceptible to eventually joining the war. While actions like that may not have prevented the United States' involvement in the war, they could have been seen as an attempt to deescalate the situation to avoid war. Second, after the attack on Pearl Harbor, FDR's administration ordered all Japanese Americans to be rounded up and sent to live in internment camps on the West Coast. That is completely racist and xenophobic, to say the least. Now, how is that different than the Nazi's use of concentration camps to eliminate their political enemies and the Jewish people during the Holocaust? Fortunately, the American people didn't murder the Japanese Americans in these camps the way the SS did to the Jewish people in Europe. But it was still persecution and wholly unamerican. If his administration was afraid of foreign spies, why did not they do the same to German Americans? That is a valid question that deserves an answer. Considering that Democrats have racist tendencies, and the Ku Klux Klan follows some of the same principles as the Nazi party did, that could explain it. Yes, Democrats were part of the KKK. But more than that, people tend to overlook what the NAZI Party acronym meant. It stood for the National Socialist Party in Germany. Now, considering that FDR's base had some support from socialists and communists, could that explain why his administration didn't treat German Americans the same way as Japanese Americans?

Next, after the German scientist Albert Einstein defected to the United States at the beginning of the war, he ordered the start of the Manhattan Project, which was tasked to construct the first atomic bomb. So, FDR and his leftist ideologues are responsible for plunging the world into the nuclear age as well. That's a decision that's made the world less safe ever since.

Finally, during the 1944 presidential election, FDR selected Harry S. Truman as his running mate. Truman may have never been president if it weren't for that. Truman was even more dangerous than FDR because of his ego. The world is still paying for the mistake of Harry S. Truman. FDR's decisions and policies put the US and the world on the brink of ruin, and only conservatism can fix it today. The US and the world would have to wait until the 1980s before those decisions were partially corrected.

CHAPTER 5

The Disastrous Legacy of
Harry S. Truman

Presidents are important figures because everything that they do sets a precedent. Now, it depends on who you talk to about former President Harry S. Truman; some consider him an all-time great and others regard him as a terribly mediocre president. But, for us to properly make that determination, we must first examine the precedents that he set while he was president and decide how those precedents affect us all today.

Now, let us use these criteria to do just that. We need to look at his popularity and biggest decisions—like the ones he used to end World War II, his economic policies, his decision to get involved in Korea militarily, and how he decided to combat communism. Having done so, you'll be able to judge for yourself what type of former President Harry S. Truman really was.

Truman is one of the most overrated presidents in American history because he constantly made crucial mistakes that affected his legacy, though many of them continue to be overlooked.

Former President Harry S. Truman's popularity has varied over the years. He wasn't immensely popular while he was in office. Truman became president in 1945 just after Franklin Delano Roosevelt had died. Even though Roosevelt picked Truman to serve as his vice-president for his fourth term, he didn't weld much power because he wasn't in the loop when it came to some of the big decisions that Roosevelt made during that time. The public might have thought that he was a placeholder for the office until the next election cycle. But for whatever reason, Harry S. Truman wasn't particularly popular. He will forever be known as the president who had the lowest job approval numbers by anyone ever to hold the office of the presidency.

Now, people today want to say that former President Trump's job approval numbers were low, but in fact, they don't even come close to Truman's. According to Real Clear Politics, Trump's approval rating was 44 percent. But Truman's job approval numbers were even with former President Richard Nixon's approval numbers, bear in mind, that followed one of the biggest political scandals of the century (i.e., Watergate). According to the American Institute of Public Opinion Records that are kept on hand at the Harry S. Truman Presidential Library, Harry S. Truman's job approval performance fell to 23 percent in 1951. Those are the average of all Gallup polls. There are many reasons why this occurred. The *main* reason is that he was both arrogant and egotistical, evidenced by the fact that he didn't listen to his advisors.

Now that we know that, we can now dive deeper into why his popularity fell in the eyes of the public. Truman's unpopularity ultimately came back to bite him and ended up affecting his legacy as president in a huge way.

Having gained a good understanding of Harry S.

Truman's unfavourability, we can now take a deeper dive into some of his decisions that created the precedent for future presidents to follow. It would be easy to start with his decision to use the atomic bombs on Japan to end World War II, but it would be better to first get a better understanding of his decisions regarding the Korean War because that area of the world is still relevant even today. So, in other words, it's fair to say that Truman's full legacy as president isn't fully decided yet. That's because his decision to get the United States involved in the war created a couple of precedents. First, Truman decided to get the United States involved in the war without congressional approval, and he did that by saying that the United States was supporting our allies in the United Nations.

In so doing, Truman violated every part of Article 1 Section 8 of the United States Constitution, which is what he used to justify his actions to start the Korean War. For example, the sixth requirement in Article 1 Section 8 was contradicted by Truman himself. That section says, "When an international body calls for the deployment of US military forces, Congress must still give its approval." That is a huge precedent to set because the United States Constitution clearly states in Article 1 Section 8 that only Congress can declare war. By him circumventing Congress, he set a dangerous precedent, which basically said that any president can go to war with another country without congressional approval by just ignoring the text of the Constitution. This did nothing but irritate Congress. The Republican-led Congress wasn't going to sit around and just let him tear up the Constitution, so they reasserted Congress' authority by passing a new law and a new constitutional amendment. Those laws alone created huge, extraordinary precedents that subsequent presidents have had to follow.

While Truman did some good things while he was president, he also did some things that upset a lot of people, which explains why he was unpopular. He was not a natural leader–rather one that was thrust into his role. Truman's popularity started declining in 1946, and later that year, Republicans took advantage and regained control of Congress. Republicans didn't like Truman whatsoever. It was kind of like how the Democrats view former President Trump today. Now, Truman was popular at the end of World War II, but he didn't have a particularly good relationship with General Douglas MacArthur. That was a huge mistake on his part because MacArthur was well-liked. MacArthur vehemently disagreed with Truman's decisions, which caused Truman to fire him. That decision alone was the biggest mistake of Truman's presidency. This was partly because Truman let his ego get the best of him, and he let the public know, too. Truman started being petty and he was quoted saying "General MacArthur was a dumb son-of-a-bitch that didn't respect the presidency." That was not true because MacArthur got along with

FDR fine, and he only took his orders from the president of the United States. The Republican-controlled Congress allowed MacArthur to speak in front of a joint session of Congress, and that's the only time that has ever occurred.

Truman's approval ratings dropped even further after that. Truman's decision to get the United States involved in the Korean War without the approval of Congress was looked down upon. Other issues that factored into the decline in former President Truman's job performance numbers were his widely unpopular economic policies and McCarthyism, which took place during the tail end of his presidency. Fair or not, Truman received wide amounts of blame and criticism for that even though Senator McCarthy was a Republican.

This paints a rather good picture of Harry S. Truman's presidency and why he was so unpopular. Truman's unpopularity and poor relationship with Congress led to the passage of laws that would forever haunt his legacy as president.

Political scientists and historians can now take a closer look at those new laws that were enacted during the Truman presidency—and the precedent they entailed. The Congress, led by Republicans, first passed the Twenty-Second Amendment, which limited the number of terms a president can serve. That amendment was able to pass partly because of Truman's unpopularity. His unpopularity led to the Republicans winning control of Congress in the 1946 mid-term elections. The Republican Party ended up controlling 246 seats in the United States House of Representatives. Meanwhile, the Republicans had won control of the United States Senates by receiving a fifty-one-seat majority. Even though the Twenty-Second Amendment received some Democrat votes in Congress, most of its support came from Republicans.

At the time, there were only forty-eight states, and thirty-six states were needed to ratify it. Some states were on the fence about the legislation. One of the states that ratified the amendment was Harry S. Truman's home state of Missouri. Although it would not have applied to Truman because he was already in office when it was passed, it essentially ended his presidency. That's because it sent a clear message that rebuked Truman. The Twenty-Second Amendment was ultimately ratified in 1951. A huge misinterpretation is that the Twenty-Second Amendment was part of FDR's legacy; if it weren't for Truman's unpopularity that led to his party losing control of Congress; it never would have passed, to begin with.

The other law that Congress eventually passed was the War Powers Resolution in 1973. This was a way for Congress to reassert its authority over the executive branch as the only branch of government that can declare war on another nation. People again misinterpret things because they tend to think that this law was in response to the Vietnam War that Presidents Kennedy and Johnson got the United

States involved in. But that is blatantly false because Congress never approved the military action that started the war. In fact, both, JFK and LBJ used the same precedent that Harry S. Truman created when he ordered the United States military to intervene in the Korean War without congressional approval. That is another huge stain on Truman's legacy as president. With the passage of the War Powers Act, Congress said that the precedent that Truman set at the beginning of the Korean War was fundamentally wrong.

Now, regardless of what you think about former President Harry S. Truman, the point about the Korean War can only be seen as a direct failure of his presidency—and the world is still witnessing the effects of that. For example, although Congress didn't like the United States' involvement one bit, but once we were involved in the war, former President Harry S. Truman had an obligation as the commander-in-chief to make sure that the United States was victorious. But he didn't do that. Instead, he let his ego and personal feelings about General Douglas MacArthur cloud his judgment, which led to him firing General MacArthur. That decision ultimately led to the stalemate that the world is witnessing today. Case and point, the Korean War never formally ended; instead, it was put on hold with an armistice, not a treaty, hence the Demilitarized Zone (DMZ).

Just look at the mess—both for North and South

Korea—that was created by Truman's arrogance and incompetence. If you want, you could even blame China's actions on Truman because he tried to help the KMT, which were part of the Chinese National Party (now residing in Taiwan) in their civil war against the communists.

Truman didn't give them enough support, however, so they got their asses kicked in that civil war. That led to China becoming a communist nation. That's vitally important because the United States would later have to fight the Chinese during the Korean War. Why? Because Truman was a pathetic leader that failed time and time again on the world stage. Why do you think that the United States gets along better with Taiwan than China? Because it's run by the KMT, whose members were exiled from China after they lost their civil war with the communists. Truman could have done several things to resolve this mess.

What could have Truman done differently? First, if he was so worried about the rise of communism throughout the world, then why not make sure the KMT defeated China after the Soviet Union tried to help the communists win? It should have been obvious that the Soviet Union was going to be an adversary of the United States after the completion of World War II. This is important because after the KMT lost their civil war, the CCP took over and became allies with the North Koreans.

Second, Truman should have done everything in

his power to prevent a war from breaking out between North Korea and the United States. Congress was content with letting the North and South Koreans solve the civil war on their own, and if the members of the United Nations wanted to get involved then so be it. But it shouldn't have ever involved the United States military. According to a memorandum titled *Blockade of North Korea*, which is kept at the Harry S. Truman Presidential Library, Truman decided to order the United States Navy to blockade North Korea in 1950 in order to prevent the communists in North Korea from receiving supplies from China. But since North Korea is landlocked with part of China, the naval blockade was perceived as a failure by Truman. Imagine what would have happened if the Truman administration would have urged the UN Security Council to impose strict economic sanctions (like the Trump administration did) while keeping the naval blockade in place. It seems that such a measure would have been the best way to proceed without going to war unnecessarily. That is an incident from which future presidents can learn. Since Truman didn't do that, General Douglas MacArthur came up with a brilliant plan to defeat the North Koreans. General MacArthur's plan was to launch a surprise invasion at Inchon, cut off their resupply lines, and drive due north toward the North Korean and Chinese border.

It was a success until the Chinese invaded the Korean peninsula. The Soviet Union backed both the

North Koreans and the Chinese. That was significant because the Soviet Union decided to copy the United States and built their own atomic bombs. Now, General MacArthur didn't care; he was willing to take them all on. MacArthur was one of the greatest generals in American history. Truman fired General MacArthur because he was too afraid of World War III breaking out. He instead chose to negotiate a peace deal after the allies had fought back to the Thirty-Eighth Parallel. Again, that was a huge mistake. People don't realize this, but there was a higher casualty rate in the Korean War than there was in the Vietnam War. Yet, Truman decided to settle for a stalemate, despite it being a war that he got the United States involved in. That is a stain on his legacy, and there's no getting around that fact.

Truman's decision to end the Korean War in a stalemate was a disaster. First, what was the purpose of the war if it didn't accomplish anything? Second, it gave tremendous amounts of credibility to both the Chinese and North Koreans. It shouldn't have mattered if the Soviet Union provided a nuclear umbrella to those two nations for one simple reason that was overlooked: they weren't and have never been credible nations when it comes to the use of nuclear weapons. There is still to this day only one nation that is, and that's the United States.

President Truman documented in his personal diary that he found out about the atomic bombs after FDR had died. When Truman was running for re-election in 1948, he spoke to a group of supporters about his decision to use the atomic bombs on Hiroshima and Nagasaki to end World War II. He was quoted saying, "It was the toughest decision that I ever had to make." But it was also the correct call because that was when the United States asserted itself on the world stage as a super-power.

Today, because of Truman, the Chinese are a powerful communist nation in search of hegemony, and North Korea is an ostracized foe that's constantly threatening to nuke the world. What could have been if the Truman administration hadn't gotten involved in nation-building? This type of globalism and liberalism has done nothing but fail time and time again. Now, the president is forced to try and clean up Truman's mess.

Harry S. Truman was one of the most overrated presidents because he set myriad disastrous precedents. Future presidents should look at him as an example of what *not* to do. His legacy will forever be diminished and tainted by controversy.

CHAPTER 6

Endless Wars

There have been numerous armed conflicts that the United States has been involved in. This is a direct result of liberalism and failed globalist policies. These failed policies date all the way back to the time that former President Woodrow Wilson was in office. The World Wars ultimately caused the Cold War as well as the armed conflicts against communism. Those conflicts included the Korean War, the Vietnam War, the Bay of Pigs incident, and the Grenada Conflict. Now, some of you may be saying, "Wait a minute. Democrats weren't solely responsible for every one of those armed conflicts. After all, former Presidents Nixon and Reagan were in charge during some of that time." This is certainly true. But the Democrats held control of Congress when Nixon and Reagan were in office, meaning that they had the power to conduct congressional oversight, and no one is considering the effects of the foreign policy conducted by Democratic presidents before them.

RINOs like the Bushes, who were in office at separate periods of time, made things even worse by getting the United States involved in armed conflicts in the Middle East. In more recent history, both Obama and Biden have made things even worse. These never-ending wars and armed conflicts are a result of nation-building and failed foreign policy that could ultimately lead to America's downfall.

The First World War was supposed to be the last of the armed conflicts around the world, but it instead became the start of nation-building that was championed by liberal globalists like former President Woodrow Wilson.

Even though the United States wanted to stay neutral in the war, the policies and the decision to send supplies on merchant ships to the British and other Allied Powers ultimately caused the United States to get involved in the Great War. That decision is on Woodrow Wilson. After the sinking of the *Lusitania*, it was just a matter of time before the United States got involved in the Great War.

The United States officially joined the First World War in 1917, but a year later, a global health pandemic hit. An argument can be made that the war helped contribute to the spread of the Spanish Flu. The Spanish Flu pandemic, along with the revolutions in the German and Russian Empires, is what ultimately triggered a negotiation to formally end the war. At the end of the First World War, former President Woodrow Wilson negotiated through the form of diplomacy a 14-point plan that created the League of Nations once the Treaty of Versailles was signed. The League of Nations was the first version of what is now called the United Nations. But the League of Nations was a disaster because the countries that originally started the First World War still didn't get along with one another. It didn't help that Woodrow Wilson's Fourteen-Point Plan and the Treaty of Versailles that his administration helped negotiate weren't ratified by Congress because they were so unpopular. That was the start of nation-building as we all know it today. It was also the cause of many future wars that the United States would later become entangled in.

World War II occurred under different circumstances. At the time the war began, the world was in the midst of the Great Depression, and the United States was in a period of isolation. But once the war started in 1939, it should have been clear that Woodrow Wilson's foreign policy had failed. But FDR still chose to carry on with the same policies, selling supplies to the Allied Powers.

After the attack on Pearl Harbor, the United States had no choice but to fight in the war. During the middle of the war, the Allies found out about the Nazi death camps and did nothing about it. Both FDR and Winston Churchill should have notified the world immediately and stated that if the Nazis didn't immediately stop those horrible atrocities, then those individuals would be tried for war crimes just like they were at Nuremberg. Another option would have been to destroy the camps to save lives in the long run. But they chose not to do that—just like they failed to call out the Soviets for their atrocities during the war. Just imagine how many lives could have been saved if they would have done something about it when they first found out.

The Allies wanted the Soviets to help fight the Germans during the war, which was a mistake. The decision to let the Soviets capture Berlin was the biggest mistake of them all. That one decision helped start the Cold War.

When former President Harry S. Truman made the decision to drop the atomic bombs on Japan, despite the objection of General MacArthur, Eisenhower, Patton, and Bradley, there was no turning back because it was the beginning of the atomic age and the arms race that occurred during the Cold War.

General Eisenhower was a RINO, and it was his decision to let the Soviets capture Berlin. So, in a way, Eisenhower is also partly to blame for the Cold War. Truman and the Allies let the Soviets annex a bunch of territory at the end of the Second World War, including parts of Southeast Asia (encompassing China and North Korea). The world is still paying for that mistake.

If there's one thing that the two world wars have in common, it's the fact that the winners of the war began nation-building. This liberal/globalist way of thinking has always been a failure because it violates a state's sovereignty. A country should never intervene in another country's business unless it directly affects its own interests. In the end, it just endangers the lives of those who serve in the military just like those who fought in Korea and Vietnam.

The Korean War was the result of former President Harry S. Truman's failures in foreign policy and weakness as a result of his appeasement strategy toward the Soviet Union. This war could have and should have been prevented, but Truman was too incompetent and weak on the world stage to do so.

Some people may say, "Wait a minute. He expressed strength by ordering the atomic bombs to be dropped on Japan, right?" But, in fact, some military leaders thought that an invasion of mainland Japan would have been a very bloody conflict, and the bombs were meant to have a psychological effect on the Japanese in order to end the Second World War, thus saving the lives of countless American servicemen. Because General Dwight D. Eisenhower allowed the Soviets to capture Berlin and reoccupy the territory it lost during the First World War, they thought that it would be okay for them to annex territory in East Asia. Truman's administration allowed them to do it. Since the Soviet Union was a communist nation, however, once they came to occupy parts of China and the northern half of the Korean peninsula, their radical ideology spread like a cancer. The United States oversaw the Allied Powers in both Europe and the Pacific, but Truman decided to appease the Soviets, which was a fatal mistake. Once those who were indoctrinated into the communist ideology invaded Korea, there was no going back, and the Korean War began.

The Korean War was a political mess from the start. It started in 1950 after the United Nations and the Truman administration stuck their noses in a situation that never should have involved them. It was a civil war between the Koreans, and the UN is supposed to use *diplomacy* to resolve conflicts. The nations that belonged to the United Nations decided instead to put boots on the ground and get involved in the armed conflict. The Truman administration decided to use that justification to get the United States military involved in another war five years after the end of the Second World War. Truman did it without congressional approval as required under the United States Constitution.

What's worse is the fact that the Korean War, at the end of the day, accomplished absolutely nothing because it ended in a stalemate. Because no treaty was signed when the fighting stopped, the war is still technically active to this day. People may not realize this, but it had a higher casualty rate than the Vietnam War and for what. Now, there is a dictator whose regime is the biggest national security threat—a man who despises the UN and the US because of their involvement in the war.

The Vietnam War was yet another political mess. It marked the first time that the United States got its ass kicked in a war, while some politicians profited, nonetheless. LBJ had ties to the defense company known as Halliburton as well as Bell Helicopter. Now, where have we heard that before? If that sounds familiar, it's because Dick Cheney had ties to Halliburton when the United States got involved in the war in Iraq. It's not right for politicians from either party to profit off the lives of US service members that have spilled their blood while serving their country—and yet they have and continue to.

Let's not forget that the Vietnam War was the most unpopular war in modern times. It also marked the first time that the United States lost a war. It was a shame because everything could have been prevented.

Both the Korean War and Vietnam War foreshadowed things to come. For example, the fall of Saigon looked awfully like the Taliban's takeover of Afghanistan in 2021. Yet, the policies initiated by Democratic presidents caused the wars in Vietnam and Korea while RINO presidents got the United States involved in armed conflicts in the Middle East. Over 58,000 Americans were killed in the Vietnam War, and countless servicemen and American POWs were left to rot after the withdrawal of troops on the ground. That is unacceptable. Any US President that gives the order to leave Americans behind after an armed military conflict is unfit to be commander in chief. RINOs and Democrats have constantly done this, and it needs to stop!!!

Nixon was president during the withdrawal from Vietnam while Jimmy Carter did nothing when Iranians took over the American embassy during his presidency, like a coward.

It got even worse than that. George H.W. Bush originally got the United States military involved in the Middle East during Operation Desert Storm and could have invaded Iraq back in the early 1990s but didn't. His son, George W. Bush, would later rectify that with the war in Iraq. Former President Bill Clinton did absolutely nothing when Osama Bin Laden and Al-Qaida originally attacked the World Trade Center. If he had hunted Osama Bin Laden down, then imagine how many lives could how been saved over the years. That's not just from the terrorist attacks on September 11, 2001, either; the attack on the *USS Cole* and the war in Afghanistan could have also been avoided. This reckless behavior got worse during Obama's presidency when his administration left brave American patriots to fend for themselves during the terrorist attack in Benghazi. Worse still, his administration paid Iranian terrorists' ransom demands just to get captured Americans back. That broke the number one rule—to never give in to terrorist demands. Now, President Joe Biden left Americans behind to get slaughtered after the troop withdrawal from Afghanistan. If the Taliban or Al-Qaida were to order another terrorist attack on the United States, which is highly likely, the United States would be back in the same position it originally was in before the War on Terror began. These wars have been nothing more than political footballs.

There are ways to handle threats and crises better. But unfortunately, these alternatives have also contributed to the endless wars the United States has been involved in. For example, at the height of the Cold War, the Castro Regime in Cuba became a national security threat by cozying up to the Soviet Union, which made JFK want to invade Cuba to prevent it. But when the Bay of Pigs incident occurred, it conveyed some weakness to the Soviets, which prompted the Cuba Missile Crisis. But JFK's administration effectively used diplomacy and MAD (Mutually Assured Destruction) to resolve the situation, though this ultimately prolonged the Cold War. Another incident that contributed to the endless wars was the Grenada conflict. Since the leaders in Grenada embraced radical Marxist ideology like the Soviets, they couldn't be trusted in the slightest. The fear of another Cuban Missile Crisis left former President Reagan little choice, so an invasion was ordered. After that, the writing was on the wall, and it was a matter of time before the Soviets were defeated in the Cold War.

If the United States had never engaged in nation-building at the start of the First World War, then all of the wars could have been prevented. All this policy does is piss off nations, inviting blowback and putting lives at risk. Wars should only be fought when absolutely necessary. Hopefully, the United States won't have to fight another war for a very long time.

CHAPTER 7

The National Debt Crisis

Over the years, the DC "Swamp" has taken over the nation's financial responsibilities and has handled them in a reckless, self-serving manner. Policies like constant government spending plans, borrowing money from hostile countries, and allowing the United States Congress to not pass a budget since the late 1990s have been the root cause of a national debt crisis. Establishment career politicians from both the Democratic and Republican Parties are to blame for this crisis. Career politicians tend to ignore the national debt because they tend to think that it could be dealt with in a timely manner, but they overlook their own involvement in the crisis.

The national debt crisis is one of the most important crises that the United States will have to deal. with because everyone's kids and grandkids will have to pay for the mistake through the form of higher taxes in order to pay off the debt. These idiotic policies have been a detriment to the country, and this crisis is sure to get worse before it gets better. Even though economic issues can be a little confusing and boring to some people, they're of crucial importance.

The middle class is the backbone of any democracy and economic issue. Economic issues drive almost every election.

Now, there may be some critics that say, "Wait a minute. Former President Bill Clinton along with the help of a Republican-controlled Congress, balanced the budget, and had a budget surplus," but that's very misleading. The budget surplus from 1998-2001 was for *public debt holdings* and not the outstanding debt owed. That's a big difference because that means that the only debt payments that were being made were those that were to the debt that was only made available to the public. It didn't prevent the federal government from borrowing additional money, and it didn't affect economic dealings with international partners. For example, the debt of companies that did business with the United Nations wasn't added to the federal debt—which makes no logical sense.

The fact that these Government-Sponsored Enterprises (GSEs) and the Treasury Department were still able to borrow money under certain circumstances led to the outstanding debt to slowly but surely increase over time. Now, how stupid and irresponsible can someone be to ever allow that to happen? Unfortunately, both the Democrats and Republicans are at fault. Congress has the power of the purse, which means they can dictate how the federal government spends money or even how debt gets paid off. Unfortunately, both, political parties are jam-packed with members that simply don't care about anyone but themselves.

In 1995, members of Congress decided that it was better for each political party to turn something like the national budget and national debt into a political football. The proof is in the pudding.

That same year when the Balanced Budget Amendment was brought up for a vote, it barely passed in the United States House of Representatives and failed in the United States Senate by one vote. That was because most Democratic lawmakers did not support it even though Bill Clinton, who was president at the time, was a Democrat, and it did not help that a few RINOs also did not support the bill. At the time, Republicans controlled the United States Senate with a fifty-three-member majority, and the Democrats had forty-seven members. But fifty-one Republican senators voted for the bill while only fourteen Democrat senators voted for the Balanced Budget Amendment.

Now, Joe Biden was one of the fourteen Democrats the supported the bill in the Senate but has since changed his mind over the years. If that bill would have passed, it had a very good chance of being ratified by three-fourths of the states needed to make it law. If the Balanced Budget Amendment had passed, then our country wouldn't be in the dire straits that they are now. Ever since then, politicians from both, political parties, stopped trusting one another and won't support any budget, government funding bill, or any bill altogether unless they have their own pet projects hidden somewhere in them. Now, how in the hell, is that okay. This is a perfect example of corruption and explains how the DC "Swamp" operates. These actions do nothing but put a burden on the average American citizen considering that it's their tax dollars that will have to pay for everything.

Throughout the years, the United States has gradually borrowed more and more money in order to finance armed conflicts throughout the world, as well as domestic projects. Shortly after former President Bill Clinton left office and George W. Bush was sworn in as the forty-third president of the United States, the terrorist attacks on September 11, 2001, occurred. That meant that the United States had to respond militarily. But what should have been a relatively short armed conflict in Afghanistan ended up lasting twenty years. But you may remember that Congress failed to pass the Balanced Budget Amendment, and the Clinton Administration never paid off the outstanding debt the United States Federal government owed, meaning that the debt continued to rise at a steady rate. To make matters worse, our government was borrowing the bulk of its money from a foreign adversary in China.

Now, considering that both George W. Bush and Bill Clinton, came from two different political parties, it's clear that both sides are to blame for this mess.

Besides, the political partisanship being played out in Washington DC, there were other mitigating factors that helped facilitate the national debt problem. For example, the armed conflicts that occurred around the world as a result of nation-building caused by the liberal globalist philosophy were just one factor that caused the United States to borrow heavily, but don't underestimate the effects that the great recession of 2008 had.

Between the War on Terrorism and the War in Iraq, the United borrowed trillions of dollars for national defense. While there's nothing wrong with that at first glance, you still must pay off your debt. The War in Iraq has always been controversial due to the fact that the government agencies behind the intelligence to go to war in Iraq were wrong from the start. Democrats try to shift their blame to Republicans for those wars because former President George W. Bush was in office and was a Republican, but let us not forget the fact that it still took Democrat votes in Congress to authorize military action for those wars. The domestic issues that arose just a year after the invasion of Iraq were a result of several devasting hurricanes that occurred from 2004-2005. The worst of which was Hurricane Katrina, which became the costliest storm in US history. This led to huge infrastructure projects that cost a lot of money, and all of that spending and borrowing put the United States in an untenable position.

By the time that former President Barrack Obama took office in 2009, the world was already in the midst of an economic crisis. Since the United States, which is the number one economy in the world, went into an economic recession in 2008 as a result of all the government spending and borrowing, the rest of the world was dragged down as well. That should have been a huge clue that the United States was struggling with the amount of debt it was taking on, but unfortunately, nothing was done about it. If the warning signs had been heeded, the United States could have prevented a national debt crisis.

There were other factors that contributed to the national debt crisis as well. First, the Obama administration was so corrupt and so incompetent that it ignored the economic and national debt situation, exacerbating the problem. For example, the Obama administration put into place economic reforms that absolutely killed small businesses in the United States while countless big corporations decided to move their companies to other countries. These economic reforms included the Affordable Care Act, the Paris Climate Accord, not approving the Keystone XL pipeline, and innumerable regulations. Critics may say that the Affordable Care Act deals with health care, not the economy, but that is flat-out wrong. This is because it mandated that employers offer health care to every employee, which is expensive for businesses. When these businesses couldn't afford to pay for health insurance for every one of their employees, they were forced to lay off workers. Businesses are at the heart of the US economy, and if they struggle financially, then the rest of the country is going to struggle financially.

The Obama administration's policies regarding climate change also killed small businesses because they were forced to entirely change how their companies conducted business in order to comply with environmental regulations. For example, tens of thousands of people were laid off when the Keystone XL pipeline was canceled. Besides the fact that those workers had to find new jobs, energy companies had to find eco-friendly ways to produce energy. These policies were incredibly stupid because it was proven during the Trump administration that the conservative approach of less government regulation, having operational oil pipelines, and not forcing businesses to make ecofriendly products creates jobs and made the United States Energy independent. When that happened, individuals had more money in their pockets to spend, which helped jump-start the economy. But the Obama/Biden administration caused the United States to sink further and further into debt because due to its irresponsible legislature.

Now, if it wasn't bad enough that Democrats and RINOs in Congress came together to make the national debt crisis even worse. They came together and voted to raise the debt limit countless times since 2008. That is just reckless and irresponsible. According to Article 1 Section 8 of the United States Constitution, Congress has "the power of the purse," which means that it can dictate how much money is spent by the federal government. Unfortunately, members of Congress have chosen to play partisan politics and relinquish their authority to the executive branch. The only time objections are raised is if the majority party in Congress is different from that of whoever controls the White House. The Founding Fathers never wanted the executive branch to control spending because it weakens the legislative branch's ability to conduct checks and balances. Because Congress has gotten lazy, the United States is now over $30 trillion dollars in debt. That has only gotten worse as a result of the COVID-19 pandemic. What's sad is the fact that it didn't have to be this way. If politicians would stop playing politics with the country's finances, the country could heal much more quickly. Congress constantly has a low approval rating, and part of the reason is how they craft spending bills. The only light at the end of the tunnel is that every time the Democrats and RINOs overreach, conservatives surge forward in the following years. Economic matters are at the heart of every issue in America, so the question is this: When will conservatives come into power to fix the debt crisis without the DC "Swamp-like creatures" in Congress screwing everything up?

CHAPTER 8

The Opioid Crisis

Over the years, tens of millions of people have become addicted to illegal drugs, including opioid painkillers. This could have been avoided if not for incompetent doctors, naive politicians, and dangerous policies like "open borders," which have been championed by Democrats. America's European allies helped cause this problem, and now, only common-sense solutions can solve it.

So, when exactly did the opioid crisis start, and who is to blame? Well, the answer is simple; the British are to blame, considering that they are the ones who started processing opium and getting other countries hooked on opium by trafficking it throughout the 1800s. One country that had enough of it was China, and this ultimately led to the Opium Wars. This is very important to understand considering that today China is a mass producer of drugs like fentanyl, which end up being trafficked to North America.

It's no secret that the Germans were using a lot of meth and cocaine during the Second World War. When the British and the other European nations learned of this, they started doing it as well. This drug use and drug trafficking then started to spiral out of control at a rate that no one could have ever predicted. Now, consider how many US service members were exposed to this, as well as how many people immigrated to the United States from Europe. You see, the Europeans have no choice but to take some responsibility for their role in causing the opioid crisis.

Naïve politicians have made the opioid crisis worse than ever. What they did was turn a blind eye to a widespread problem. So, since when is it okay for an elected official, who is accountable to the people, to be lazy and ignore a problem that endangers their constituents?

This level of incompetence dates all the way back to the early 1900s when Calvin Coolidge appointed J. Edgar Hoover to be the director of the Federal Bureau of Investigations. That's important because J. Edgar Hoover refused to admit that the Mafia existed. The mafia established the French Connection, which was a major drug supply line between the United States and Europe. There were huge amounts of heroin and other narcotics being poured into the United States by the Italian mafia. By the time the FBI realized that this was a problem, it was too late because people were already hooked on drugs. This was just further evidence of how our European allies and corrupt politicians from both sides of the aisle helped cause this massive problem.

As if naïve politicians didn't cause enough damage to the United States by ignoring the enormous drug problem, they now have begun to let states legalize marijuana use. Now, that is just stupid. Marijuana is nothing more than a gateway drug to the more hardcore drugs, plain and simple. Most of the states that have legalized marijuana are solid-blue states like California, Oregon, Washington, New York, and Illinois. Red states, on the other hand, aren't willing to go this far. Ruby-red states like South Carlina, Wyoming, Tennessee, and Idaho absolutely refuse to legalize marijuana (even for medicinal purposes) because they understand the ramifications of that decision. But unfortunately, not all red states are like this. For example, both Montana and Alaska have fully legalized marijuana in part because both states have a lot of libertarians that don't like to be told how to live their lives. Even solid-red states such as Alabama, Mississippi, and Arkansas have legalized marijuana for medicinal purposes because Republican leaders in those states lacked the courage and the will to take a stand against laws like that. RINOs from those states are part of the problem because they are the ones that lack the courage to do the right thing. But do not for a second underestimate the effect money plays throughout this whole process. Lobbying firms will throw money at politicians up for re-election just to buy their vote for laws like this, and states are making a fortune off the American people as a result of this reckless policy of the legalization process. Politicians like these RINOs have no principles because they have shown time and time again that they are willing to sell their souls and votes regardless of the policy. This is a perfect example of how the "Swamp" works.

Doctors, themselves, have contributed to the

opioid crisis as well. For example, doctors will often prescribe drugs like morphine and sometimes low amounts of fentanyl to combat pain after a patient has surgery. They will also sometimes pre-scribe pain killers like oxycodone for the same reason. While there is nothing wrong with a doctor giving a patient something for pain, the problem is that if patients aren't properly weaned off these potent painkillers, then they can become addicted to them. When that happens, addicts will keep going back to the doctor complaining of pain in order to get their prescriptions renewed.

Now, pharmacies keep track of drugs like Sudafed because some of its ingredients can also be used to make meth. So, the question must be asked, if pharmacies can track someone's purchases of Sudafed to prevent meth labs from popping up all over the place, then why can't they also track how many times someone has a prescription for high-powered painkillers renewed? You would think that such a precautionary measure would help reduce the number of people that are addicted to opioids. Another problem that arises from patients not being prop-erly weaned off medication is that when those who have become addicted to them can no longer get them from their doctors, then they will turn to the streets for a fix. Illegal drugs like heroin, meth, and fentanyl can quickly replace drugs like morphine and oxycodone, which is extremely danger-ous, to say the least. Democrats and RINOs alike have failed to realize that point.

Drug cartels quickly moved to fill the painkiller void by supplying these addicts. They started moving large amounts of meth, heroin, and fentanyl into the United States. This was all made possible because of a lenient border-security policy. Over the years, Democrats have weaponized the border issue against Republican lawmakers in order to appeal to Hispanics and win over the Latino vote in elections, and RINOs conceded that and refused to stop it. While Democrats and Republicans have been busy arguing with one another about the border policy, drug cartels have been taking advantage of the situation. You see, drug cartels scope out weak spots along the border (of which there are plenty), disguising themselves in migrant caravans and using mules to transport their drugs into the country. The mules that the cartels use are the most significant since they can hide the drugs and travel almost anywhere throughout the country via car, ship, or plane. While federal law enforcement agencies, like the DEA, US Customs and Border Patrol, TSA, and ICE, tend to catch a fair amount of people attempting to smuggle drugs into the United States, they can't possibly catch everyone. The cartels know that, too. These drug cartels originate primarily in Central and South American countries like Panama, Guatemala, and Columbia. Tens of millions of Americans have been affected by these reckless policies. As a result, at least 453,000

Americans died from 1999-2016 from overdoses of opioid medication, and that isn't including deaths from overdoses of illegal substitute drugs like heroin and fentanyl. Just to put that into context, there have been over 750,000 recorded deaths in the United States as a result of the COVID-19 pandemic. So, the fact that nothing has been done to stop the opioid pandemic is astonishing.

There is supposed to be an education program in place in order to teach kids about the effects of illicit drugs to prevent them from both using and becoming addicted to them. That program is called the DARE program, which stands for Drug Abuse Resistance Education. It was founded in the 1980s around the time that former President Ronald Reagan declared a war on drugs. The DARE program was always intended to be a preventative measure, and it stayed like that until 2007. Shortly after the Obama administration came into power, however, the Democrats forced critical race theory into the schools and turned the DARE program into an issue of race instead of a preventative measure. The proof is that the curriculum for the Dare program shifted its focus from educating the effects of illegal drugs in order to prevent kids from using them to behavioral issues.

This issue is too important and should never have been politicized/racially manipulated. The foremost issue should always be to save lives. People are dying in the streets from overdoses, and the Democrats turn it into an issue of race. That just speaks to their level of incompetence. Since the COVID-19 pandemic started, the DARE program has been in shambles, struggling to survive. But without proper education, the American people will continue to struggle with the consequences of the opioid pandemic.

CHAPTER 9

Operation "Crossfire Hurricane"

Although there have been corrupt politicians before, nothing challenges the amount of corruption that was displayed during the Obama administration. Now, some might say, "What about the corruption that was revealed by former President Richard Nixon during the Watergate scandal?" Unfortunately, Watergate was relatively small compared to Operation "Crossfire Hurricane." While they both involve spying on a rival political campaign during a presidential election, the amount of government agencies and foreign actors involved doesn't even compare. The mainstream media and Big Tech helped cover up the political scandal known as Operation "Crossfire Hurricane." Partisan politics and the complexity of the operation itself have made it even more difficult for the average person to comprehend what truly happened.

Operation "Crossfire Hurricane" was conceived shortly after the Hillary Clinton e-mail scandal was uncovered. It was announced by former FBI director James Comey that former Secretary of State Hillary Clinton was under investigation for her use of a (since destroyed) private e-mail server that was also connected to the Democratic National Convention being hacked during the 2016 presidential election. This is important because when she served the Obama administration as secretary of state, she wasn't authorized to use a private e-mail server to conduct official business nor is any other government official since it is not a secure form of communication. While the investigation shouldn't have been political in nature, this quickly changed when former President Bill Clinton met with former US Attorney General Lorretta Lynch on a tarmac to discuss it. That never should have been allowed, and after the meeting, Lorretta Lynch overruled former FBI director James Comey in bringing charges against her and called it an unfortunate "matter." That was after James Comey held a press conference in July 2016 where he stated that Hillary Clinton was involved in gross negligence with the handling of a private e-mail server since multiple foreign adversaries could have hacked her account during that time period. This is exactly the reason why the Clinton campaign, Democratic National Convention, and the DC "Swamp" made up and put into motion Operation "Crossfire Hurricane." You see, they wanted to make the Clinton e-mail scandal go away, and this was their insurance policy to do so. That gives them motive to engage in this level of corruption. It's completely unacceptable and unconscionable that they would have the gall to even conceive such a thing.

The Clinton campaign developed the notion that the Trump campaign was concluding with Russians to defeat her campaign and win the presidency. That was completely fallacious, and they knew it, too. Yet, Hillary Clinton knew that after those accusations had been made publicly, the FBI would have no choice but to investigate it. It also served another purpose, carrying a built-in excuse if her campaign lost to Donald Trump. Now, since the political establishment from both parties as well as the DC "Swamp" bureaucrats absolutely hated Donald Trump and everything he stood for because they knew that he would bring change and disrupt what they do, they went along with the story known as Trump/Russia collusion. The Clinton campaign used the DNC to contract Fusion GPS to conduct opposition research on Donald Trump. This was significant for two reasons. First, Fusion GPS employed Nellie Ohr, who was the wife of Bruce Ohr. Bruce Ohr was a high-ranking employee for the Department of Justice. So, do you honestly believe that a married couple, with the careers that they had, never discussed what they did for work during their off time? Second, Fusion GPS decided to hire former British spy Christopher Steele, who ended up concocting the fake Trump Dossier, which was full of lies. Fusion GPS then had Christopher Steele sell that lie to the FBI and Clinton Campaign. You truly can't make this stuff up. Since the Ohrs were involved with both, this lie should have stopped there, but it didn't. That is a shame.

Hillary Clinton's presidential campaign was fully aware of what was going on at Fusion GPS and the Department of Justice. That's because the Clinton campaign employed Jake Sullivan as a foreign policy advisor. Now, if that name sounds familiar, it's because he's the very same person that President Joe Biden picked to be his national security advisor.

Jake Sullivan had contacts with Igor Danchenko and Michael Sussmann. Igor Danchenko was a Russian national that helped feed some of the fake stories about Donald Trump to Christopher Steele. Michael Sussmann was the attorney for the Clinton campaign who helped negotiate the funding of Christopher Steele's Trump Dossier with the help of a Russian bank. So, once again, the Democrats were guilty of something that they accused a Republican of. Hillary Clinton's presidential campaign was the one guilty of colluding with the Russians during the 2016 presidential campaign, not Donald Trump's. This was made abundantly clear after Special Counsel John Durham indicted both Igor Danchenko and Michael Sussmann for their wrongdoings while also naming Jake Sullivan in one of the indictments. Michael Sussman was later tried and found not guilty for his alleged part of feeding the FBI false information from the fake Trump dossier by a corrupt DC jury. No one else has yet to go on trial for their alleged crimes. Durham is hoping that justice will ultimately prevail, but he is fighting the D.C. "Swamp" from all sides. He is especially fighting a corrupt DOJ and Attorney General, who is loyal only to President Biden and not the rule of law, that have the ability to overrule him at any time. These corrupt acts need to stop!!!

Unfortunately, the corruption didn't stop there. The Department of Justice and FBI agents investigating the Clinton campaign's allegation of Donald

Trump colluding with the Russians to defeat her took the fake Trump Dossier to heart. From there, those corrupt agents took their bias and disdain for Donald Trump to the next level, and they went and lied to the FISA court in order to attain a FISA warrant for Carter Page, who was a low-level advisor for the Trump campaign. But, in order to get a FISA warrant to monitor Carter Page, the FBI had to include the made-up Trump Dossier authored by Christopher Steele. What makes that even worse is the fact that the FBI could not verify the information in the dossier. Hell, Christopher Steele couldn't verify the information in his own dossier. Former FBI Director James Comey's memos state that the Trump dossier couldn't be verified. To make matters even worse, the FBI never once warned Donald Trump about a potential foreign agent trying to infiltrate his presidential campaign. It is a crime to lie in court and to law enforcement, so with that being said, how in the hell did the FBI agents tasked with investigating the Clinton campaign's allegation get away with lying to a FISA court? That is a valid question that demands an answer.

Former United States Attorney General Lorretta Lynch is the only person that could have authorized such an investigation. That's because the FISA would have had to be signed by the US attorney general. Another critical question that deserves an answer is this: If the FBI knew that the Trump dossier couldn't be verified, then why was the damn thing even taken to the FISA court, to begin with? The answer is that the FBI and DOJ investigators hated Donald Trump. According to Department of Justice Inspector General Michael Horowitz, the FBI never would have been able to attain a FISA warrant against Carter Page without the fake Trump dossier. That meant that there was no probable cause to attain any warrant, yet one was approved anyway.

One final but major question must be asked: What did former President Barrack Obama know and when did he know it? It's fair to ask, considering that former Attorney General Lorretta Lynch was a cabinet member in the Obama administration. Are you naïve enough to believe that the president of the United States wasn't briefed about a presidential candidate of a major political party being under investigation for possibly colluding with foreign spies? No, he would have been briefed at some point. So, how far did this conspiracy reach? Well, that answer is connected to Carter Page's profession.

Now, Carter Page was an asset for the Central Intelligence Agency, and for that reason, former CIA Director John Brennan had to know that Carter Page was a target of Operation "Crossfire Hurricane" and let it happen. If the CIA was fully aware of the Trump dossier and Russian collusion allegations, then it is plausible that the rest of the intelligence community was aware as well. So, if the intelligence community knew that former MI6 official Christopher Steele had an agenda to damage Donald Trump, then why would they put out an official statement to dis-credit both him and his dossier unless they also had an agenda to politicize and weaponize it against the Trump campaign? Former CIA Director John Brennan, former DNI Director James Clapper, and former FBI Director James Comey went to the White House and briefed the President of the United States about the situation. The American people now know this briefing took place after former FBI Agent Peter Strozok and lawyer Lisa Page's text messages were released to the public and reported by Fox News. This was done for three possible reasons. First, since it involved a major political party candidate for president and a foreign national, it was seen as an issue of national security, about which the President of the United States should have been briefed. Second, this briefing was only meant as a check in the box, so that everyone involved in Operation "Crossfire Hurricane" could attempt to cover their own ass. Finally, as the leader of the Democratic party, former President Barrack Obama helped the Clinton campaign fabricate this scam because of his disdain for Donald Trump, and he wanted an update. That doesn't require a stretch of the imagination. If all of these government agencies and officials were engaged in such a conspiracy, then that is a crime—namely, *treason*.

Unfortunately, this is not the first time in American history that this has happened. Former President Richard Nixon and former Vice President

Spiro Agnew were once accused of spying on a political campaign and placed under federal investigation by the FBI. Richard Nixon received a presidential pardon from former President Gerald Ford for his involvement in the Watergate Scandal. So, here is a valid question: What is the difference (if any) between the Watergate Scandal and Operation "Crossfire Hurricane?" The answer is that, at first glance, there isn't much difference, but once you start to peel back the onion a bit, you quickly see that Operation "Crossfire Hurricane" was much larger than Watergate, and the mainstream media, as well as Big Tech, helped cover it up.

Once the fake Trump dossier was released to the media, they ran with it and never looked back. That's because the mainstream media is run by registered Democrats. Hell, just take a moment to look at some of the so-called news anchors on some of these cable news networks. For example, over at ABC News, George Stephanopoulos, who was an advisor to former President Bill Clinton, is anchoring *Good Morning America* while over at CNN, you had Chris Cuomo, who is the brother of former New York Democrat Governor Andrew Cuomo. When you have individuals that clearly lean toward and favor one side of the ideological spectrum, how can anyone honestly expect them to remain neutral and fair as honest journalists are supposed to be?

Critics will say, "What about shows hosted by the likes of Sean Hannity and Tucker Carlson over at Fox News?" Well, the answer is yes, those shows do lean to the right and yes, they are opinionated, but the difference is that the hosts at Fox News are upfront about their opinions instead of reporting them as facts.

Another example of media bias is over at MSNBC News where Al Sharpton, who tries to inject race into everything, is employed while other networks like CNN let Don Lemmon, who does the same thing, anchor a show in a primetime slot. This is important to mention because it paints a picture of the mainstream media's bias. Their bias became even more evident in the way that the fake Trump dossier and Russia collusion investigation were covered.

After the Hillary Clinton presidential campaign accused Donald Trump of colluding with the Russians, the mainstream media ran with it hook, line, and sinker. They did it because they hated Donald Trump and still do to this very day. But why are people not surprised considering that once the Trump dossier was leaked to the media, they used it to convict Donald Trump in the court of public opinion? After Donald Trump beat Hillary Clinton fair and square in the election, they still refused to give him credit. After former Special Counsel Robert Mueller was appointed to investigate the allegations, the mainstream media still reported that Donald Trump was guilty. There was no due process given by the media.

And they didn't stop there. MSNBC News hired

former CIA director John Brennan while CNN hired former DNI director James Clapper as political commentators. It truly boggles the mind. The decision to hire both of those individuals was incredibly reckless and irresponsible–especially if you consider the fact that both individuals were directly involved in the Mueller investigation and shouldn't have been commenting on it anyways. But then again, the Democrats think that rules don't apply to them.

Even after the Mueller Investigation concluded and the report was made available to the public, the media still tried to demonize former President Donald Trump by saying that the Mueller Report stated that he tried to obstruct the Mueller probe by threatening to fire him, thus making him guilty of obstruction of justice. That was nothing more than a Democrat talking point and a flat-out lie.

The media's bias toward Democrats was shown yet again. They completely glossed over some of the main points because they didn't fit their narrative. For instance, the Mueller Report states that "the investigation did not establish that members of the Trump Campaign conspired or coordinated with the Russian government in its election interference activities." That is a direct quote from the Mueller Report, and it's also the most significant. That means that Donald Trump didn't collude with the Russians in order to beat Hillary Clinton. Furthermore, the report determined that no votes were altered. So again, that means that Donald Trump beat Hillary Clinton fair and square in the 2016 presidential election, but the media glossed over these crucial points and let their own bias get the better of them.

All the while, news networks like MSNBC News, CNN, and ABC News allowed Congressman Adam Schiff and Congressman Eric Swalwell to spew Democrat talking points and lies when they were both members of the House Intelligence Committee and should have known better. Next, the mainstream also polished over the legal point that if there wasn't a conspiracy or underlining crime committed connected directly to Donald Trump, then there couldn't be any obstruction of justice, especially since he never fired Robert Mueller or impeded his investigation. Robert Mueller, himself, wasn't sure, so he left that decision to the United States Attorney General, who decided that there was no obstruction of justice. But the media just didn't care. Finally, the media gave a pass to the Big Tech companies over their gross incompetence found in the Mueller Report. The Mueller probe found that Russian entities used websites such as *Facebook*, *Google*, *Twitter*, and *YouTube*, creating fake accounts in order to spread disinformation and create political unrest throughout the United States. But again, the media overlooked it because those companies are run by billionaires that donate to the Democratic Party. The public will never trust the media and Big Tech again if they continue to be dishonest like they were with their handling of Operation "Crossfire Hurricane" reporting.

Now, Special Counsel John Durham is tasked with getting to the bottom of the origins of the Operation "Crossfire Hurricane" probe. The question now remains: will anyone be held accountable for what occurred in a way that still allows them due process? Unless those who were involved in corrupt acts within the federal government face consequences, there can never be equal justice under the law.

Finally, how can corruption like this be prevented from happening again? Until those questions are answered, this country will always be at risk of government corruption, which is something the Founding Fathers always feared. But with the indictments from John Durham's probe being made public, there is hope that this type of corruption can indeed be prevented from happening in the future.

CHAPTER 10

The Lincoln Project

During former President Donald Trump's term, a bunch of RINOs, who absolutely hated him and everything that he stood for, formed a group known as The Lincoln Project. It was being portrayed by the group of RINOs and the media as a group of Republicans that was going to return the Republican party to greatness by embracing the values of Abraham Lincoln. But this group of "Never Trumpers" had flawed concepts and were part of the DC "Swamp." They also got played like a fiddle by the Democrats during the 2020 presidential election. These RINOs betrayed their own political party in order to advance their own selfish need, but in doing so, they brought the entire country to the brink of ruin.

The group of Trump-hating RINOs that composed the Lincoln Project spent a lot of time in the mainstream media spewing their hatred at the Trump administration. But this was allowed to happen because it fit the media's narrative. What's worse is the fact that every one of the founding members of the Lincoln Project was still called a Republican even though they had left the Republican Party, and most of them decided to register as Democrats. This just speaks to the mainstream media's dishonesty. This group of people was supposed to be standing up for Republican principles, which they clearly didn't believe in, as they switched political parties at the first chance, they got. This is the reason why they're called RINOs. Now, one of these Never Trumpers is

Steve Schmidt, who was hired by MSNBC News to be a political commentator and attack Donald Trump. This hatred of Donald Trump, the double standards, and media bias has helped put these Never Trumpers on the path that they're on today.

In 2019, the RINOs led by Steve Schmidt and seven other individuals formed the Lincoln Project with the sole purpose of preventing Donald Trump from winning another term in office as President of the United States in the 2020 election. A key question that deserves an answer is this: How can anyone still be identified as a Republican if they are actively campaigning against both a Republican president and candidates for Congress who support him? The answer is that they *can't*. The members who formed the Lincoln Project don't care about anyone but themselves. All they care about is how can they get back into power and make backroom deals that only benefit themselves and their friends. That is how the DC "Swamp" works, but until someone has the guts to call them out on it, it will never change. The proof was put on display when Steve Schmidt, George Conway, and the other five founding members of the Lincoln Project allowed John Weaver to also join the group when it was originally founded even though they probably knew about the scandal he was mixed up in. In 2020, John Weaver was accused of sexual harassment by granting political favors in exchange for sex with at least ten different men and one fourteen-year-old. That is just sick and disgusting. John Weaver later admitted to the first part of the allegation but not the second. But has anything ever come of it like? Was there ever a police investigation or anything close to it? The answer is no. Why is that? Could it be the fact that John Weaver was close friends with the McCain family, the Bush family, Senator Mitt Romney, and former Ohio Governor John Kasich? Now, every one of those individuals hated Donald Trump as well, but more importantly, they all ran national campaigns for president, and the Bush family had two former presidents within its ranks. That means that John Weaver's friends had the power to cover up his scandal and minimize the damage if they thought it was going to be an embarrassment to them because of their relationships with him. They all had political connections to do it. You see, the Lincoln Project and the "Never Trumpers" didn't give a damn about anyone but themselves because if they did, John Weaver would have been investigated even after he resigned from the Lincoln Project. With all of this, there are two more crucial questions that deserve answers. First, if a sex scandal can either end or cripple most political campaigns, then how is that the Lincoln Project was still able to operate? Second, why wasn't the mainstream media covering that story properly and why haven't they ever followed up? The answer to both is that the DC "Swamp" looks after its own regardless of party affiliation, and the media is full of "Swamp-like creatures" as well. The Lincoln Project can also counter and spin its own narrative of stories with Steve Schmidt working at MSNBC. This is because unless it fits their narrative they don't care, and it's only gotten worse since then.

During the 2020 presidential election, the Lincoln Project actively campaigned against former President Donald Trump and every Republican politician who supported him. That was even after the Democrats started touting socialist policies like defund the police, court packing, open borders, and the Green New Deal climate change initiatives, all the while actively campaigning against capitalism. No true conservative would ever support those types of policies because it would ruin the country by putting it just one step away from becoming a communist nation. Yet, the Lincoln Project and "Never Trumpers" not only campaigned against Republicans because of their hatred for Donald Trump, but they also publicly endorsed Democrat candidates like Joe Biden. Their justification for it was to purge Donald Trump and anyone who supported him from the Republican Party. These "Never Trumpers" and members of the Lincoln Project are not principle-based conservatives because they're blinded by their hatred of one person. Even after former President Donald Trump left office, you would have thought that the Lincoln Project and their media allies run by Democrats would have said "mission accomplished" and ceased the rest of their campaign and organization against Trump and conservatives who continued to support him, but they didn't. Why is that? That's because they fear him running again in 2024 and his likely winning with ease. This was evident when the Lincoln Project actively campaigned against Governor Glenn Youngkin in Virginia's gubernatorial race in 2021. That was a place where the Republicans hadn't won a statewide election in twelve years, so you would have thought that the members of the Lincoln Project would have supported a Republican candidate that had a realistic chance of winning there. But they didn't, which represents further proof that they are just RINOs, not true conservatives.

During the Virginia gubernatorial race, the Lincoln Project tried to recreate the Charlottesville Incident by paying college students to act like white supremacists that were campaigning with Glenn Youngkin. The mainstream media turned on them then, yet when they had an accused pedophile among their ranks, the media scarcely reported the matter. This just shows what kind of sick and disgusting levels they are willing to go to in order to express their hatred of Donald Trump. When will this sordid behavior stop? Only when the mainstream media goes back to basic unbiased reporting and start acting like honest journalists.

The Lincoln Project has caused more damage to this country than they will ever know. They showed just how powerful and corrupt the DC "Swamp" really is.

Because they infiltrated the mainstream media, they have a huge platform to spew their hatred and bias. Therefore, the term fake news came to light because the American people can see right through it.

Consequently, the trust in media is at an all-time low. Just imagine what this country would look like if the Lincoln Project decided not to be petty and throw a childish temper tantrum. Would the Democrats be in control of Congress and the White House? Would there be open borders where illegal drugs and human trafficking are being promoted? Would there be record-high inflation? Would the United States be in such unprecedented danger of attacks from abroad? Once you answer those questions, you can see the damage that the Lincoln Project has helped create.

The question at this point: How do fix this mess? The answer: We need patriotic Americans willing to take a stand and get involved by either running for political office, even in a small capacity (e.g., school board staff, local mayor, sheriff, etc.) or entering careers like college professors or news reporters and bring back balance to the system. In this manner, the American people can exact the change that is so desperately needed. That is the conservative way and how a true conservative movement takes shape. Unfortunately, the RINOs that run the Lincoln Project have never understood that concept. Conservatism is the only way this mess can be fixed.

CHAPTER 11
The Exploitation of a Global Pandemic

The Democratic Party used the COVID-19 pandemic as a smokescreen so that they could force radical socialism on the American people. This was done through multiple means, but it primarily occurred through the lockdown measures, which were exploited for their own private gain.

As these exploitations of this pandemic are explored, one must ask how sick these people are to perpetrate such deceptive fraud. The sad thing is that it could have all been prevented if the Democrats weren't so greedy and power hungry. The COVID-19 pandemic turned into a highly volatile political issue when it didn't need to be. But in order to fully understand what happened minus the politics, one must look at the timeline of events. Then and only then can the world finally understand how this deadly pandemic occurred so that we could learn from it in order to prevent another global health pandemic.

The COVID-19 pandemic started when the first case of coronavirus was reported in the Wuhan Provence of Hubei, China, on November 17, 2019. The place where the COVID-19 pandemic started is highly significant because it is the same location where a Chinese laboratory is located. That Chinese laboratory was the Wuhan Institute of Virology. Now, this same laboratory has a sketchy past, and it was also reported that it was conducting experiments on coronaviruses from bats to see if they were capable of infecting humans by binding to the human ACE2 receptor. But, in order to do this, the Chinese virologists used mice for their experiments to mimic humans. Now, if that sounds an awful lot like gain-of-function research. That's because it is. What's worse is the fact that the United States National Institute of Allergy and Infectious Diseases (NIAID), which is run by Dr. Anthony Fauci, who is also a physician for the United States National Institute of Health (NIH), helped fund this research. So, that means that the National Institute of Health and especially Dr. Fauci knew about COVID-19 well before it turned into a global pandemic that spread like a wildfire. But, instead of coming clean to the rest of the world, Dr. Fauci, the NIH, and the Chinese communist government decided that it would be better to try and cover it up and protect their own asses. How many lives could have been saved if it weren't for them? And this was just the beginning. It turned political before it ever reached the United States.

In December 2019, the Democrats in the United States House of Representatives decided to impeach Donald Trump for a highly partisan and political issue regarding a phone call with the leader of Ukraine. But please look at the date. The first reported case of COVID-19 occurred in China in November 2019, so by engaging in a partisan impeachment that cost the US taxpayers a great deal of money just to hurt him politically, they also caused an unnecessary distraction that likely made the COVID-19 pandemic even worse. So, in other words, the Democrats chose to play politics at the beginning of the pandemic, and they haven't stopped playing politics since then. That means that the Democratic Party has blood on its hands when it comes to the amount of people that have died from the Covid-19 pandemic as a result of their political games. Unfortunately, this was just the beginning of how political the global pandemic would become.

While he was still in office, former President Donald Trump had to make many crucial decisions in order to protect every American. One of those decisions was to ban travel from China and other European nations. As usual, the Democrats turned the decision into a political football. Why did they do that? The Democrats decided to play political games throughout the pandemic because it was in the middle of the 2020 presidential election. For them to do that just to secure enough votes to win an election and not to do the right thing is just sick and disgusting. Joe Biden started it off by stating that the ban on China was xenophobic and racist. But we shouldn't be surprised considering that if the Democrats don't like something, then they immediately call it racist and play identity politics. Never mind the fact that the virus originated in China and at the time there were cases being reported in Europe.

The Democrats also disliked the fact that Donald Trump and the Republican Party started referring to the COVID-19 pandemic as the "China Virus" because it originated in China. But again, the Democrats cried foul and said that it was xenophobic and racist. It wasn't until all fifty state governors had to make critical decisions regarding the pandemic and even meet with Donald Trump virtually to ask for federal aid that they eased their political attacks. The lockdowns would only make the politicization of the coronavirus pandemic worse.

The coronavirus became a global issue when the World Health Organization (WHO) officially designated it a global pandemic on March 11, 2020. There were also signs that the world would suffer economically and possibly go into a global economic recession. The day after the WHO classified the COVID-19 virus as a pandemic, the global stock markets took a nosedive, which only complicated the political situation further. The Democrats thought that they smelled blood in the water, and they saw an opportunity to attack former President Donald Trump for being irresponsible and incompetent. That was a flat-out lie, and they knew it too. But unfortunately, all the Democrats saw was the world in a global pandemic and a Republican president in office whom they absolutely hated and deemed weakened after a partisan impeachment, so they went on the attack saying that Democrats could handle the situation better. That is just sick and disgusting. No wonder people don't trust career politicians because they don't care about anyone but themselves.

Now, former President Donald Trump created Operation Warp Speed on March 15, 2020, which was four days after the WHO declared the virus a global pandemic. That is highly significant because it helped save countless lives. But after the advice of doctors at the NIH and CDC like Dr. Anthony Fauci, the Trump Administration asked the country to stay home for fifteen days, so that the hospitals nationwide wouldn't be overrun. This was known as "fifteen days to slow the spread," but once again the Democrats saw an opportunity to fulfill their lust for political power. One of the biggest myths regarding the pandemic is that the federal government shut everything down, but most of the fifty states shut down on their own when their governors ordered the lockdowns at the advice of the CDC. In fact, there were some states that never ordered lockdowns—like South Dakota and Nebraska. States like Georgia were criticized by the media for opening everything up after just fifteen days. But those states are red states and governed mostly by conservatives, and this is where the political divide over COVID-19 became noticeable to the American people. The pandemic was worse off in blue states like New York, New Jersey, Washington, and California. The way Democrats handled the pandemic in blue states made the political divide even worse, simultaneously putting lives at risk.

Blue states wanted to criticize how former President Donald Trump and the federal government responded to the coronavirus pandemic, but they made it worse by playing politics. For example, when states like New York and California told the federal government that their first responders, doctors, and nurses lacked proper protective equipment (PPE) and that their hospitals lacked ventilators, former President Donald Trump enacted the Defense Production Act, which required businesses like General Motors to work with the military to produce materials needed during times of crises. In this case, it was to produce enough PPE and medical supplies needed to combat the pandemic. Donald Trump even ordered the military to transport these materials to each of the fifty states. Now, that sounds an awful lot like presidential leadership and what the president of the United States is supposed to do during times of crisis. (Never mind the fact that after the 9/11 terrorist attacks and the anthrax scare in the early 2000s, each state should have followed the recommendation of the federal government to have enough ventilators and PPE just in case to combat future crises.) So, why didn't those states—especially New York—heed that recommendation and have enough supplies on hand? That is a valid question, considering the fact that New York has been a target that terrorists have attacked for decades. Both New York and California have massive populations of citizens. But Democrats don't think like that whatsoever. Instead of planning for the worst and hoping for the best (the way a responsible government official would do), they chose to do the opposite. When the hospitals in blue states like California and New York were overrun, Trump sent the *USNS Comfort* to New York City and the *USNS Mercy* to Los Angeles, and he ordered the military to put up MASH units to help take the load off the hospitals in those states.

Governor Gavin Newsom of California and former (now disgraced) Governor Andrew Cuomo of New York said thank you to Donald Trump for sending those resources to their states. But they barely used them because they were afraid that there would have been bad optics for them and favorable press for Donald Trump for his handling of the pandemic, which the Democrats absolutely did not want. That's because the Democrats were so vindictive that they would rather play political games in the middle of a global health pandemic just so they could try to paint their political rival as incompetent rather than doing the right thing in order to save lives. Now, how in the hell is that right? They even dismissed using therapeutics to help combat the virus all because Dr. Fauci said "the science" didn't back them up, even though they'd been proven to work in several countries."

Dr. Fauci has been wrong time and time again. Let's not forget that he knew about the virus from the beginning. But why be surprised considering the Democrats loved the lockdowns and restrictive measures because they realized that they could exploit them by pushing through their socialist agenda.

In the spring of 2020, former President Donald Trump started holding campaign rallies again but only outside. This absolutely enraged the Democrats and their allies in the mainstream media, who labeled it reckless behavior. They said that these tens of thousands of people gathering outside were "super spreader events" for the coronavirus. But little did they know that they were about to contradict themselves in a major way.

On May 25, 2020, George Floyd was killed during an attempt to arrest him for attempting to pay for something in a store with a counterfeit $20 bill, which is a felony. That incident kicked off the riots during the summer of 2020 that were orchestrated by Black Lives Matter and ANTIFA, whom most conservatives view as domestic terrorist organizations just like the Ku Klux Klan. In every major city, there were thousands of people rioting, looting, and trying to hurt police officers. But did the Democratic Party and their allies in the media condemn these actions? The answer to that question is an unequivocal: "Hell No." They instead tried to cover for these bad actors by calling them peaceful protests when there wasn't anything peaceful about them. So why did they do that? It's because the Democrats saw this as an opportunity to placate the black community in order to solidify the black vote in the 2020 general election. That's it; the Democrats were willing to watch their own cities burn just so that they could play identity politics to win the minority vote. That is just sick and disgusting. But notice the fact that the Democrats or the allies in the media never once said that the thousands of individuals gathering in the streets of every major city during a global health pandemic were super spreader events like they did for those who attended Trump's rallies. That is proof that the Democrats just wanted to scare everyone and use the pandemic as a ploy for their own benefit.

Most Americans don't support defunding the police, and yet the Democrats embraced it. The media refused to call them out because they were getting the ratings. It was the democratic socialists led by the "Squad," which was led by United States Congresswoman Alexandria Ocasio-Cortez (AOC) and United States Senator Bernie Sanders, who pushed for this radicalized socialist policy to become mainstream within the Democratic Party. But instead of the leaders of the Democratic Party standing up to these individuals, they gave them even more power to enact even more radicalized socialist policies.

During the midst of the 2020 riots, the Democrats fully embraced "Cancel Culture" and the 1619 Project that was being taught in schools. So, how do we know this? Well, the proof is when statues of historical figures started to get destroyed and taken down during the riots, as well as teachers ultimately embracing the Black Lives Movement and the LGBTQ community. Teachers in school districts like that of Loudon County, Virginia started ridiculing students if they didn't support those policies. They even took it a step further and put BLM and pride flags inside the schools and classrooms, weaving those policies into the curriculum being taught to students. Now, it looks pretty clear that the Democrats were trying to force the schools to indoctrinate every student in order to get them to think like them and support the same policies they do. Students that didn't conform would be ridiculed and berated until their parents removed that student from school. Once again, you can't make this stuff up!!!

As much as people may want to, you can't erase history. Critical Race Theory shouldn't be taught to kids under any circumstances. But just as bad as all of this is, it got even worse when every single school district across America closed (and went virtual) during the COVID-19 lockdowns. Some teachers got lazy and didn't want to even return to work once the lockdowns were lifted, using COVID-19 as an excuse. Schools nationwide imposed draconian measures, which they said were to prevent COVID-19 outbreaks. Those measures included mask mandates, social distancing, mandatory testing of COVID-19, and even mandatory vaccines once they became available. These school districts denied religious exemptions to students who wanted to protest those restrictive measures. This violates their First and Fourteenth Amendment Rights, yet these schools did it anyway, as they simply didn't care.

Now, the Democrats saw what these school districts were doing and opted to try to impose policies nationally. That's because they knew that the teachers' union was a major donor to their party. They also knew that the teachers' union didn't have the guts to stand up to them. The only silver lining is that during the COVID-19 lockdown, parents started paying just a little more attention to their kids' education and learned about what their kids were being taught in schools. This pissed them off to no end. It started to come to a head when Glenn Youngkin was elected Governor of Virginia. But what is happening in the schools is only part of the Democrats' ultimate plan to achieve absolute power.

Toward the end of 2020 with the general election near, the Democrats decided to push for mail-in ballots to ensure that there weren't huge crowds of people while voting. While it's a good idea in theory, it spells disaster for future elections. For example, Republicans tend to like to vote in person on election day, while Democrats usually tend to lead the early vote and absentee vote. That means that the Democrats would have a clear advantage in future elections. Now, critics will say that Republican-controlled states allowed mail-in voting to occur in the 2020 general election, but that's misleading. Republicans allowed absentee voting—with *caveats*. Those caveats included requiring a voter to present photo ID and using signature verification for people to request a bal-lot. Furthermore, the Republican-controlled states, for the most part, put in place strict deadlines for those ballots to be received and counted, and those deadlines were set for the day of the election. The Democrats obviously cried foul and slammed it as voter suppression. Blue states generally mailed out ballots to every registered voter whether they requested a ballot or not. The state of California is a perfect example of this. About a week after the election, it was determined that Joe Biden had won the presidency and the Democrats had won complete control of the United States Congress. You see, that is far too long to determine the outcome of an election, especially when one party had a clear advantage over the other. All it did was create mistrust. There were even reports that those who opted to vote in person were required to wear face masks and show proof that they had tested negative for COVID-19 when there was no such requirement for elections. Those who chose not to comply with those orders said that some polling workers tried to turn them away and deny them their right to vote.

These events preceded the events that occurred on January 6, 2021. Now, regardless of your politics or feelings about that day, people tend to overlook the few key questions that deserve answers. First, why did those individuals do what they did? Second, after the riots of 2020, why wasn't the national guard and capitol police placed on standby just in case, when they knew that a giant rally was scheduled to take place in Washington, DC, that day? Finally, did those individuals even vote in the election? Those are valid questions that deserve answers.

It was determined that former President Donald Trump received over seventy-four million votes in the 2020 presidential election. The dumbasses that chose to go into the capital building on January 6 did it because they believed the election was stolen and not fair. Those individuals were labeled as Trump supporters. Let's just lowball it and say that 15 percent of Trump's supporters thought the same thing; that's still over eleven million people. So, are you willing to say that that's healthy for our democracy? The answer is an unequivocal no.

The Democrats along with a few RINOs that never liked Donald Trump opted to impeach him for a second time because of what some people did. But COVID-19 was still a problem, and he would have been out of office in a few weeks anyway. So, the Democrats and the RINOs that went along with that have even more blood on their hands when it comes to COVID-19-related deaths. These events only made COVID-19 a bigger problem.

Since Joe Biden has taken office as president of the United States, the pandemic has lingered. Some might even say that President Biden has even made the situation even worse in America as a result of his disastrous policies. Before leaving office, Donald

Trump's administration left Joe Biden's administration with not one but two vaccines, with another just waiting for approval by the FDA—all thanks to Operation Warp Speed. There were also therapeutic medications to be used, infrastructure in place to distribute, and another vaccine that was used by other countries even though it wasn't FDA approved in the United States.

So, what has President Biden's administration done to improve on that success? Not a damn thing. Joe Biden's incompetence has led to him invoking policies like open borders, which makes everyone less safe. Is his administration requiring proof of negative Covid tests from migrants at the border before releasing these individuals into American society? No, he's not. Does that policy endanger other countries? Yes, it does because in many cases, the migrants are traveling through multiple countries just to reach the United States.

President Biden has chosen to force the vaccine onto the American people against their will by mandating it. The Biden administration is requiring that the Occupational Safety and Health Administration (OSHA) put in place a federal mandate that requires employers to demand that employees are fully vaccinated for COVID-19 or face termination. That's been a colossal mistake and has faced widespread backlash since being announced. It's forced the military to discharge personnel and police forces in crime-ridden cities to downsize even further, thus creating a worker shortage. Moreover, the Biden administration has created a supply chain crisis in the middle of the COVID-19 pandemic by not letting supply ships dock and unload their cargo since there aren't enough workers to unload the cargo ship as a result of his policies. This has done nothing but cause the United States to hit the highest level of inflation in thirty-nine years. As if that weren't enough, there have been more COVID-19 deaths in 2021 under the Biden administration than there ever were in 2020 under the Trump administration. That's according to John Hopkins University. Joe Biden promised to end the COVID-19 pandemic during his campaign in 2020, but he has failed miserably. The average American just wants to live their lives without the government telling them how to do it and try to return to some type of normalcy.

To quote Donald Trump, "You can't make the cure worse than the virus itself." The question now: How much longer will the American people and the rest of the world have to deal with the virus before we put it behind us by making smart choices?

EPILOGUE

This was a story about how over time the Democratic Party and a few RINOs damaged this great nation and brought it to its knees with their policies. It was also a story about the history of corruption. In total, it shows us how selfish certain politicians can be in order to maintain their power and standing. It shows that America's will and foundations are still strong, and that just one person can indeed enact change for the better if they're willing to take a stand—just like the way Abraham Lincoln changed things.

Conservative principles were used throughout this story to show the difference between the policies enacted by Democrats, a few select RINOs, and Republicans. America was founded as a center-right country, and that is still true today. Just because most conservatives today are associated with the Republican Party, don't be mistaken; that wasn't always the case. Conservatism is a philosophy and practice meant to keep big government off the little guy's back. People should be able to have philosophical differences and still get along with one another. Unfortunately, that isn't the case today.

This story wasn't written to show that one political party or ideology is better than the other. No, that isn't the intent. The intent is to educate the average American citizen, who may not be aware of how dangerous some of the policies laid out in this book are, so they can formulate their own informed opinions. That refers to individualism, which is at the heart of the conservative principles this country was founded upon.

The other reason for this story is to prevent the United States from ever becoming a socialist or communist nation, as nothing could more surely spell the nation's ruin. Sadly, we're on the very cusp of this nightmarish reality—and it's something that most Americans don't want.

The only question that now remains: Just what do *you* believe in?

www.ingramcontent.com/pod-product-compliance
Lightning Source LLC
Chambersburg PA
CBHW070253290326
41930CB00041B/2509